Quality at Work in
Research and Development

George J. Kidd, Jr.

QUALITY RESOURCES
A Division of The Kraus Organization Limited
White Plains, New York

Most Quality Resources books are available at quantity discounts when purchased in bulk. For more information contact:

Special Sales Department
Quality Resources
A Division of The Kraus Organization Limited
One Water Street
White Plains, New York 10601
800-247-8519   914-761-9600

Printed in the United States of America

96 95 94 93 92   10 9 8 7 6 5 4 3 2 1

Quality Resources
A Division of The Kraus Organization Limited
One Water Street
White Plains, New York 10601

The paper used in this publication meets the minimum requirements of American National Standard for Information Sciences—Permanence of Paper for Printed Library Materials, ANSI Z39.48-1984.

ISBN 0-527-91655-2

Library of Congress Cataloging-in-Publication Data
Kidd, George J.
    Quality at work in research and development / George J. Kidd, Jr.
      p. cm.
    Includes bibliographical references and index.
    ISBN 0-527-91655-2 (alk. paper)
    1. Research, Industrial—Quality control. I. Title.
    T175.K43 1992
    658.5'7—dc20   92-8864
                                                      CIP

Contents

Preface

A little over 20 years ago, a growing interest in crafts led to my involvement in the creation of a craft guild. The people involved wanted it to be a respected organization, and they realized that future members should be selected on the basis of the quality of their workmanship. I was selected to head the standards committee and take care of the selection process. The questions and answers that evolved from that activity started what has been my continuing interest in quality and has led to the creation of this book.

When the company for which I work changed management in 1985, a new, more formal approach to quality was instituted. This was due in part to the fact that our company's prime "customer," the U.S. Department of Energy, began to require more structured quality plans and evaluations; there also was a more formal tradition of quality in the new parent company. When I went to the literature to locate available material, I found that there was very little information available and that the "state of the art" was just in its infancy. My conclusion was that many aspects of the field still were being defined, and that the applicability and usefulness of quality tools and techniques to various aspects of industry still was being debated.

Over the years, I continued to ponder the question of how to judge the quality of crafts. My professional activities during this period began with work as a researcher in the area of heat transfer, fluid mechanics, and thermodynamics, and evolved into managing a variety of technical organizations. The conjunction of an amateur's interest in quality and a professional's need for answers to an administrative predicament is what got me started exploring how to develop a quality program that would apply to the technical endeavors that I now was responsible for managing.

Initially, I went to the literature to find out what information was already available; then, I joined the American Society for Quality Control (ASQC) and attended its meetings to meet the individuals active in the field. I began to develop my own ideas, and tried them out first in the organization I managed. As the concepts matured and were validated in my organization, I wrote papers on the subject and submitted them for peer review. Now that I have an understanding of the subject and believe I have some original contributions to make, I am writing this book to share these insights with my colleagues. The concept of the *system*, which is fundamental to the understanding of thermodynamics and many other technical disciplines, forms the basis of the approach to quality activities described in this book.

Any activity that spans a quarter of a century involves many people, too many to acknowledge individually. A few individuals and groups, however, have been especially influential in guiding my thinking and I would like to mention them. My interest in things technical came from two uncles. My uncle Emerson Houts was a classic example of a rural American mechanic; he owned a bottled gas distributorship in Michigan and could build anything and everything. Some of my favorite memories are captured on movie film—my cousins and I riding in a home-made car powered by a gasoline washing machine engine that my uncle and older cousins constructed. The other uncle, W. E. (Willy) Konold, was an engineer who was employed by the phone company. He worked at the Hawthorne plant of Western Electric during the 1920s and was associated with Dr. J. R. Juran for a period. Uncle Willy's home was a treasure house of technical toys, from ham radio equipment to a handmade speedboat. My professional career was influenced most by Dr. Robert L. Young, who not only taught me thermodynamics, but also taught me a great deal about the fun of technology. In my personal growth, the Reverend Joseph Boulet helped me develop the strength to try out new ideas and to learn to enjoy working with people. In terms of groups, I first want to recognize my co-workers and managers in Oak Ridge who served as guinea pigs and encouraged and supported me and, second, to recognize the many people who helped with the creation of this book, especially Thomas Tallant of Martin Marietta Energy Systems, Inc., and the team at Quality Resources. I also would like to thank J. W. Zolyniak, G. K. Werner, and B. S. Lankford for their help with some of the figures. Finally, I owe my greatest debt to my family—parents, wife, and children—who nurtured me not only during the writing of this book, but in the years leading up to it.

Chapter **1**

Introduction

The application of quality tools and techniques is not widespread in the research and development (R&D) community. I believe the primary reasons for this are a lack of understanding of how to apply these tools and techniques to research and development activities and the lack of ways to assess the effects of a quality program in a research and development organization. To put it another way, we do not seem to know what to do, how to do it, or how to tell if we have been successful when we are done. The goals of this book are to show what can be done, how to do it, and how to evaluate the results.

Since its inception in the late 1920s, the quality field has been directed primarily to the manufacturing world. The statistical tools developed and implemented at that time had significant impact on the then-emerging mass-production method of manufacturing, and have continued to serve it well over the years. It has been only in the last 20 years that the number and types of tools available and their sophistication have increased. The range of applications also has expanded greatly over that period, from an almost exclusive emphasis on examination of finished subassemblies and products, to attention to the processes that produce those outputs, to recognition of the importance of the goods and services that go into the processes. There also has been an increased awareness of the importance of the "customer's" requirements on the determination of the quality of goods and services.

Accompanying this expansion of the range of interest in manufacturing activities, two other shifts in emphasis have occurred in recent years. First, the scope of application of quality tools and techniques has started to spread to other functions in manufacturing companies as people realize that purchasing, engineering, maintenance, field service, and so forth have an impact on the total quality of the delivered output. These broadened perspectives have appeared under such concepts as total quality management (TQM) and quality function deployment (QFD).

Second, in this same general time frame the range of application has expanded to include other industries. Among the first to be affected were the construction and fabrication industries. Emphasis on doing things right the first time and the use of consensus standards characterized the approach in these fields. More recently, attention is starting to be directed toward some parts of the service industry, for example, the communications, utilities, banking, and hotel sectors.

Time for Application to Knowledge Work

The time has come for these trends to expand into the arena of knowledge work, which encompasses such diverse activities as research, development, design, law, art, and literature (1–3). Many companies are realizing the importance of good design, based on sound research and development work, to the ultimate quality of the products they produce or the services they provide. It is probably not unreasonable that the areas of research and development have been late in getting attention. While they now are being recognized as some of the most important areas, they are also among the most difficult to characterize and to evaluate.

Each phase of the expansions described above has met naturally with a set of growing pains. As the quality field expanded from manufacturing into new areas, the first attempts at developing quality programs were based on the use of existing tools and techniques, either in their present form or slightly modified, in the new applications. In some cases, this was successful; in others it failed and new concepts had to be developed and tested. For example, statistical methods are proving to be quite useful in some repetitive service applications, but have limited value in the construction industry. In another area, a recent paper argues that human factor engineering methods are more significant than statistical methods in the operation of nuclear power plants (4).

At the same time these changes were taking place, managers were beginning to realize the technical and economic impact that research, development, design, and testing activities have on the eventual success of goods and services in the marketplace. Although we now seem to be at the point at which we appreciate the nature of the situation, our understanding of the mechanisms and interactions involved in the translation of science and technology into products and services still is limited. Nevertheless, it is obvious that the adage, "garbage in, garbage out," applies to product life cycles just as it does to computer operations; the better we can make our science and technology, the better our goods and services will be.

Resistance to Change

When any new idea is introduced into a culture, there is generally an initial period of skepticism and reluctance to accept the idea. Much of this reluctance stems from a simple fear of the unknown. For example, consider the introduction of the personal computer to the management culture. There was, and to some extent still is, a resistance by managers to using personal computers in their jobs. This reluctance comes from not wanting to spend the time, money, and effort to acquire the "newfangled" hardware and then learn to use it. This is accompanied by uncertainty about whether this new machine actually will be a help rather than an additional burden, and the managers' fear that they will not be able to use it well and that contemporaries will be one up on them.

Ultimately, acceptance of any new concept is aided by two factors: seeing and understanding how the concept will be useful, and developing the skills to employ it. The main challenges in introducing quality into research and development are to show the benefits of a quality program and then to explain how to use the "tools of the trade"; in other words, how to make the program user-friendly.

A salesperson who starts out to introduce a new product into a new territory, if he or she is any good, will take some time to understand what kind of resistance to expect so that an appropriate strategy to overcome the resistance can be developed. If the basis for the resistance seems to be well founded, perhaps the product should be changed. To paraphrase current thinking in the quality field, the salesperson needs to talk to the potential customers to find out what they want and need, and also understand what they don't think they want. As we consider introducing quality principles and techniques into the research and development territory, my experience has shown that, as a general rule, it is safe to assume that technical people, like almost everyone else, resist new administrative requirements. This is especially true when they perceive these requirements will have little value to them or their work. The reason for this is simply that their time is limited, and they would rather work on technical matters than administrative chores. Most people who have spent four years or more learning to do technical work are not comfortable doing administrative tasks. They have not had much training in these areas and feel awkward performing such tasks. More than that, they *like* technical work. Most of the people I know working in research and development preferred science to English in school and they liked calculus better than accounting. There are a few of us who have discovered that management actually can be fun, but I suspect we are relatively few and far between.

In addition, people engaged in research and development contend that the output of research and development is too subjective to measure in any meaningful way (5,6). Also, the average scientist will argue that the basic nature of research is to discover the truth, and that quality considerations are not needed in addition to what they already do. The benefit of a quality program is to provide a degree of discipline in what often is considered by outsiders to be a disordered process.

The difficulty comes from the very nature of the creative process. In many activities, the outcome can be related directly to the inputs. Consider one of the common examples given to illustrate the positive aspects of a quality improvement program, that of replacing a machine in a factory. Presumably, we have historical data on the existing machine's characteristics and understand its capability for producing some number of items at a certain rate with a known maintenance cost. We also know its value as used equipment. Therefore, the cost per part using this machine can be calculated fairly accurately. If a new machine is put in its place, it will have similar factors, and the cost for the new machine also can be calculated. The decision about replacing the old machine is then quite simple, at least in theory. If the new machine is cheaper than the old, buy the new one. Decision makers like this type of situation. However, even in this relatively simple case, there are additional factors to consider. Unless the new machine is exactly like the old one, there are likely to be training costs, or at least a learning period, associated with the new equipment. Further, if the new item is from a different manufacturer, there are likely to be "acceptance" issues associated with it. Users of equipment, whether they are in the shop or in the laboratory, often develop strong product loyalties. While these can be equated to ease of use and other somewhat quantifiable parameters, they are generally more subjective, and relate to such things as ease of finding information in manuals, assistance from service organizations, and how well the unit fits the space available.

It is little wonder then that the research and development community will assert that the measurement of quality in their field is virtually impossible and, therefore, that decisions cannot and should not be made on the basis of quality. However, all decisions are made on some basis, rational or not, valid or not, objective or not, and once this is recognized and accepted then the idea of quality can be used as a powerful tool to assist in the decision-making process at all levels, from picking new instruments, to selecting staff members, to allocating limited funds among research proposals.

The research and development world also rewards people primarily for their technical accomplishments, not their administrative accomplishments. Technical people also resent having outsiders involved in the evaluation of their work. My alter ego in the craft world has taught me that woodworkers prefer to have their work judged by other woodworkers. So it is no wonder that the folks in the laboratories are going to be apprehensive when they hear that they are going to have to participate in what they are apt to perceive as the company's latest management fad.

However, just as most managers (myself included) have come to understand, appreciate, and even like the use of computers in their jobs, I believe that the same ultimately will be true for the use of quality tools in research and development. One of the ironies of the situation is that the quality profession developed as a result of the application of the statistical methods devised for analyzing experimental data for manufacturing applications. The concept is now about to make a full circle.

An Approach to Quality

This book presents an approach to quality from the point of view of a scientist turned manager. As I put the material for this book together and reflected on the maturity of the quality profession, I formed the opinion that the profession is moving from a collection of somewhat disjointed ideas and techniques to a unified science. The thermal sciences were in the same condition 140 years ago. As Myron Tribus (a thermodynamicist turned manager and quality advocate) points out in his book on the thermal sciences, "The difficulty which troubled our forbears prior to 1850 was that these energy methods of analysis seemed to work only in special cases" (7, p. xv).

In slightly over 60 years since the publication of Shewhart's book on the application of statistical techniques to quality control in manufacturing, the quality profession has been able to make major contributions to the quality of manufactured goods and do it in a cost-effective manner (8,9). Quality programs in manufacturing usually are based heavily on the use of statistics and on a system of auditing to assure compliance with quality control procedures. To be certified as a quality engineer by the ASQC, a candidate must demonstrate competence in these areas as well as in the field of metrology and a variety of relevant management areas (10). This approach has provided and will continue to provide consumers with safe, reliable, low-maintenance products at competitive prices. However, there are shortcomings to this philosophy when attempts are made to apply it in other fields, especially those fields in which the number of items produced is small, the tangibility of the product is low, or both. It is my opinion that these shortcomings can be mitigated by the development of a global view of quality activities.

In this book, I present some general quality methods and then show how they can be used to solve problems in a yet-unsolved special quality case, research and development. The book is intended for people doing research and development, managers of research and development organizations, and quality professionals associated with such organizations. It also should be of interest and use to teachers in universities, and those involved with training and consulting organizations that work with the research and development community.

The primary purpose of the book is to give people engaged in research and development a guide to practical tools that they can use to improve the real quality and perceived quality of their work. Secondary purposes are to provide the upper-level managers, supervisors, and other professionals who work directly with technical staffs, a framework for understanding the nature of research and development and how it fits into the whole fabric of a company.

This is not a handbook. Research and development cannot be done by the book; similarly, a quality program for a research or development organization cannot be done by the book. Rather, it is a guidebook; as anyone who has ever read a technical textbook knows, the details are left to the reader. In writing the book, the approach I took was to start with first principles insofar as possible. It is my opinion that many of the problems associated with deploying quality principles to areas other than traditional manufacturing are a result of giving the answers before the proper questions are asked. In applying quality, as in doing any technical work, it is important that the worker understand the basic principles involved and not jump in and try to apply a solution developed for one situation in another situation in which it is not appropriate.

When anyone needs to solve a technical problem in applied mathematics for the first time, it is important to go back to the basic governing equations and determine which terms are significant and which can be neglected. So it is with the application of quality techniques: one must examine the entire system involved and then, and only then, can the correct techniques for analysis be developed. In technology, the worker has a variety of tools at his or her disposal, ranging from handbook solutions for common problems already solved and cataloged, to powerful analytical techniques and computer programs for describing the most complex systems. Similarly, in the quality field, the practitioner has tools ranging from the straightforward application of well-developed techniques and procedures for manufacturing applications to new ideas about the application of sophisticated matrix analysis methods for exploring the problems of complex service environments. I describe a comprehensive system model that includes all the factors playing a part in a quality system and then focus on those of particular significance to the technical community.

References

1. M. G. Beruvides and D. J. Sumanth, "Knowledge Work: A Conceptual Analysis and Structure," in *Productivity Management Frontiers—I*, ed. D. J. Sumanth (Amsterdam: Elsevier Science Publishers B. V., 1987), 127–89.

2. Robert E. Kelley, "Managing the New Workforce," *Machine Design* 62(9):109–13 (May 1990).

3. Robert E. Kelley, *The Gold-Collar Worker: Harnessing the Brainpower of the New Work Force* (Reading, MA: Addison-Wesley), 1985.

4. Raymond S. Markowski, "Defining the Quality Professional in the Nuclear Utility Industry," *Energy Update* 10(1):5 (March 1990).

5. Dennis R. Arter, "Why NQA-1 Will Not Work for Research," *Proceedings of the Thirteenth Annual National Energy Division Conference*, Fort Lauderdale, FL, September 21–24, 1986, C 1.1–1.7.

6. Roy H. Williams and Ronald M. Zigli, "Ambiguity Impedes Quality in the Service Industries," *Quality Progress* 16(10): 14–17 (July 1987).

7. Myron Tribus, *Thermostatics and Thermodynamics: An Introduction to Energy, Information and States of Matter, with Engineering Applications* (Princeton, NJ: Van Nostrand, 1961).

8. W. A. Shewhart, *Economic Control of Quality of Manufactured Product* (New York: D. Van Nostrand, 1931).

9. Philip B. Crosby, *Quality Is Free: The Art of Making Quality Certain* (New York: McGraw-Hill, 1979).

10. American Society for Quality Control, *Certification, Quality Engineer: Quality Engineer in Training* (Milwaukee, WI: ASQC, July 1989).

Chapter 2

The Idea of Quality

The concept of quality is probably as old as humankind. When people began to keep written records, they gave indications that they were concerned about the quality of their work. A drawing from early Egypt shows a measurement being taken of a large stone, probably a building block. The interpretation of the drawing is that a check was being made of some dimension to be sure the stone was in conformance to a standard; one of the major organizations in the quality field uses this drawing in its logo today.

In this section, I briefly trace the growth, from the earliest times to the present, of the concept of quality as a property of a good or service. (The material on very early times, of course, is necessarily speculative.) The Juran Foundation is preparing a comprehensive history of the quality field that should be available in its entirety within a few years, and Cox and Garvin present interesting summaries of developments in the 18th and 19th centuries (1–3).

In the earliest of times, society was composed of hunter–gatherers, and the constant search for food, shelter, and safety dominated their lives. Material possessions were scarce. The idea of an item's fitness for intended use must have been domi-

nant, and the producer and consumer were the same. If someone needed a spear, that person made it and only had to satisfy
himself or herself. The concept of standards was rudimentary
and must have been based on comparisons with the implements
of others in the group. Purposes for tools and other implements
were straightforward. However, even at this stage in human development, the idea of something above minimum standards for
utility existed. This took two forms: ornamentation, and the use
of special or select materials.

With the growth of farming and the division of labor that
this allowed, the creation of many of the implements of every-
day life now was done by specialists, the craftspeople. Initially,
the producer and customer were known to each other and the
transactions must have been similar to those between a craftsperson and a buyer at a contemporary craft show. The craftsperson was aware that, in order to remain in business and in
good standing in the community, the quality of his or her work
must be satisfactory (4). The buyer, on the other hand, now was
put in the position of having to be able to judge the quality of
the goods to be acquired. This system has persisted for some
items up to the present time. Small, locally owned businesses
that employ a few workers, such as bakeries, wineries, custom
tailors, and potters, are typical examples.

The next major change came about as a result of increased
prosperity, which led to the further division of labor, which in
turn led to the first form of manufacturing. Small items were
made mostly by the individual and larger items were made under the supervision of a master craftsperson. There was also a
subtle change in the distribution of goods as general stores began to supplement the specialty shop of the craftsperson. As the
number of individuals between producer and consumer increased, the need for quality control became evident. There are,
I believe, two basic reasons for this. First, a natural and inno-
cent disparity exists between the expectations of suppliers and
those of consumers. Second, some people have a tendency to
be lax about conforming to someone else's requirements, especially when they are not likely to be called to task for producing
output of lower quality than desired.

The Emergence of Formal Standards

In the Western world, the formal definition of standards seems to have begun during the Middle Ages along with the growth of commerce and a general recognition of the need for rules of national conduct. Many governments in that period enforced very strict standards for the composition and fabrication of goods (5).

Even before these formal standards came into being, examples exist in early writings of edicts concerning quality. The concept of self-imposed standards seems to have come later, the most notable example being the guilds that evolved in medieval Europe (6). It was toward the end of this era that two of the most profound technological events in our history occurred: the replacement of animal and natural (wind and water) energy sources with mechanical energy sources, and the beginning of modern science.

The final factor in our history of quality is the introduction of mass production. The early instances of mass production were accomplished with animal (including manual) or natural energy, but the availability of mechanical energy accelerated its application so that, within the span of roughly half a century, this method of manufacturing became the leading form of production for most consumer goods. Mass production had four effects on our culture: (1) it reduced the cost of manufactured goods (along with a lot of help from the expanding fields of science); (2) it increased the number and variety of items available; (3) it diffused the responsibility for each item produced; and (4) it lengthened the span from the consumer to a now more nebulous producer. These changes in manufacturing in turn had an impact on the distribution system. Instead of a craftsperson selling wares at the shop where the items were produced, a whole network of wholesalers and general stores developed, further isolating the consumer from the producer. These factors combined to cause manufacturers to seek better means of controlling the quality of their products, which led to the beginnings of the formal concept of quality as something that can be measured and controlled in the manufacturing process.

During most of human history, the average individual has

had very few possessions compared with those of modern consumers. Only in the last 50 years has a major segment of the population other than the ruling class had ready access to a large quantity and variety of goods.

As a result of these changes in society, two effects are beginning to surface. First, as our level of sophistication increases, we want to apply the quality lessons and benefits derived in the last few years in mass-production environments to more portions of the industrial world. Second, we expect the level of the standards used to determine quality to increase steadily with time. As competition increases around the world, those countries with the ability to produce items or deliver services at higher standards than others enjoy significant advantages over their competition.

History Repeats Itself

It is interesting to reflect on the significance of quality to individuals and groups engaged in research and development in light of the historical development of the topic. Since antiquity, the individual who produced an item or service was the one most concerned about the quality of the thing that individual used or provided. This perspective really has not changed over the years. Even though financial requirements and formal environmental, health, and safety standards have been imposed on some aspects of technical work, as far as the technical specialists are concerned, they are still the ones who have to be satisfied first with the technical content of the work. Indeed, technical results generally will not see the light of day until the producer is happy. (This occasionally leads to other problems, as with perfectionists who will not make their data available to others in an organization until they have gone over them one more time.) As the scientific community grew, so did the need for internal standards similar in function to those created by the medieval craft guilds. Finally, the techniques developed by the technical world to quantify the validity of their experimental results are being used extensively in the manufacturing world to quantify the accuracy of the parts produced.

The current situation concerning the quality of science and technology parallels the perspectives that have developed about quality over the centuries. In the type of work research and development workers perform, the first and foremost individual to be satisfied is the worker. Then, the interaction between the producer and the "client" must be considered, as it always has been. The relationship between the research or development worker and the scientific and technical community is similar to that of the craftsperson and the guild of the Middle Ages. In both cases, the professional community serves as an overseer of the general quality of the products created by the individual members. The task now is to carry this tradition forward in a rational and productive manner.

Today, much research and development is sponsored by government, universities, and large companies and is viewed by the sponsors and the public as being similar to mass-produced goods. Sponsors and the public apparently would like to have a "quality control" department that could make some easily understood measurements and thereby distinguish good research from bad, and also prevent any current or future damage to health and the environment. Unfortunately, the easy things to measure, such as the pounds of papers written (pluses) or pounds of waste generated (minuses), have little to do with the quality of the work accomplished. While some people always will want to take an easy route to evaluation, this book demonstrates a better way that organizations in the research and development community can use internally to satisfy themselves that their work is appropriate and fit for its intended use. The techniques described also allow the technical community to demonstrate that the sponsors are getting what they paid for and that the work is being done in a responsible and conscientious manner.

Recent Developments

By the beginning of the 20th century, two developments had brought about a change in the way quality of manufactured items was managed. First, the physical and psychological distance between the producer and receiver had increased. Second, the cost of checking the quality of subassemblies, assemblies, and finished goods had grown. The public still expected satisfactory quality in the goods they purchased, and for the most part manufacturers wanted to produce good-quality merchandise at a reasonable price. These factors drove one of the country's largest manufacturers to seek methods for controlling the cost of its inspection process. This search lead to the development of what has become statistical quality control. The first comprehensive definition of this methodology was in the book, *Economic Control of Quality of Manufactured Product*, by W. A. Shewhart of the Bell Laboratories (7). These concepts then were put into practice in the Hawthorne plant of the manufacturing arm of the Bell System, Western Electric. In his book, Shewhart defines control as follows: "For our present purpose a phenomenon will be said to be controlled when, through the use of past experience, we can predict, at least within limits, how the phenomenon may be expected to vary in the future. Here it is understood that prediction within limits means that we can state, at least approximately, the probability that the observed phenomenon will fall within the given limits" (7, p. 6). The basic idea is that one need not inspect every item being manufactured, but only a small sample, provided the process producing the items is under control.

This concept has been extremely useful in the manufacturing world and has led to an increasing level of quality in the manufactured items produced all over the world. By the end of World War II, the quality field had matured to the point at which a national organization, the ASQC, was formed in the United States, an organization that has grown to over 80,000 members in its first 50 years of existence.

However, in recent years the technology in use around the world has become so complex, and the consequences of mistakes so great, that the need for attention to quality has expanded significantly. As the cost and complexity of large manufacturing and power plants has increased and their potential harmful impact on their surroundings has been realized, the need to ensure the quality of all aspects of their operation has magnified. Indeed, the quality profession has recognized the need to expand its scope of interest to all phases of industry rather than just the control of the quality of manufactured items. As the scope expands, the quality profession is in a state of flux wherein its basic missions are being expanded and much of the existing terminology is being redefined and new terms are being coined.

The Emergence of Quality as a Science

Studying the history of most scientific fields shows that the early history of a science is made up largely of uncoordinated empirical observations. The next phase usually consists of attempts to fit these pieces together into some cohesive pattern. Often the available body of knowledge is confused by inaccurate observations or erroneous conclusions about some of the data. This confusion can slow down progress for years as workers in the field try to make theories fit information that is not valid.

The field of quality, in my opinion, is in the early stages of its scientific development. In the mature phase of a science, a unified theory should emerge to put all the pieces of the puzzle in place and show how the different parts relate to one another. A comprehensive perspective in a science will show how special cases fit into the bigger picture and which simplifying assumptions lead to what special cases. Until that level of understanding is achieved, a problem can arise when one attempts to use an approach based on a unique set of simplifying assumptions for other situations in which these assumptions are not valid. At present, practitioners seem to be attempting to use tools and techniques developed for an application in one area for radically different applications in other areas. In particular, attempts are being made to use analytical tools that were developed for use in manufacturing environments (in which the outputs have many objective measures) to service environments (in which the outputs are characterized principally by subjective measures).

As is the case in other sciences, professionals in the quality field are recognizing the problems and raising the relevant issues. However, because the technology is in its infancy, they still are unable to offer specific answers. Once a science has matured, a competent worker can and should develop solutions for new problems from first principles. This book is an attempt to bring a bit of unified theory to the science of quality and show how a few basic principles can be used in the application to science.

The Meaning of Quality

When quality principles developed for use in the manufacturing industries are introduced into such a new area as research and development, the people who will be affected are uncertain about the meaning of what is probably a new terminology to them. Too often, quality concepts are introduced to an organization without an adequate explanation of what is meant by the new terms and how the application of the unfamiliar concepts will affect the organization. There is a legitimate concern that the program will be just another exercise in generating paper and will wind up being detrimental rather than productive. I believe that many of the concepts of a quality program, properly defined, are inherent in research and development. As a result, a quality program will help focus the activities of the technical staff and in the long run will improve the effectiveness and value of the information produced. Here, I deal only with the concept of quality itself.

The word "quality" has a wide variety of legitimate definitions in the vernacular, and writers in the quality literature have proposed such other definitions as "fitness for use" (8, p. 1). Other authors have used a multifaceted approach to the definition of quality based on philosophical, economic, market, and management points of view (9). One attempt at a standard definition, promulgated by the International Organization for Standardization (ISO), is "the totality of features and characteristics of a product or service that bear on its ability to satisfy stated or implied needs" (10, p. 2).

The Quality Field

One use of the word "quality" is to characterize a field of study or a professional discipline. For this case, I define it as the activities dealing with the preparation, execution, evaluation, improvement, and correction of goods and services. As such, quality is a branch of management along with finance, personnel, planning, and safety. Each of these fields has a body of knowledge associated with it, the principles are taught in schools, and there are professional societies devoted to the exchange of information relating to the field. Quality has quality control, quality assurance (QA), and quality auditing as subdivisions. Just as there are such personnel tools as performance appraisal, so too there are quality tools. Just as a company has a financial program, it has (or, at least, should have) a quality program.

Quality as a Property

The second use of the word "quality" is to designate a characteristic of a good or service. Quality in this sense is a derived property: one that cannot be measured directly, but must be derived from other measurable properties. The most common way of determining the quality of an item is to compare its dimensions with a predetermined value of some parameter, usually referred to as a standard. Here, we use the term "dimension" in its most general sense, as the value of any property of the good or service. As such, it includes not only the geometric dimensions of the entity, but also could include its physical, chemical, electrical, social, or aesthetic properties. The standard therefore must be expressed in the same units as the parameter under consideration. With physical objects, this is a fairly straightforward process. An object should be of a certain size, color, and weight. An automobile engine should deliver a certain amount of power at a given speed and for certain specific fuel consumptions. A machine tool should operate so many hours between failures, and so on. Perhaps the most difficult part of establishing the quality is determining what standard (or standards) should be used.

For tangible items, the properties that determine the quality normally can be described clearly and can be measured objectively, even though the measurement may be complex and difficult to perform. In this situation, quality can be thought of in the classical terms of conformance to standards or requirements. One can think of standards as physical dimensions and requirements as performance measures. However, when dealing with services, the standards and requirements are more subjective and therefore more difficult to quantify. The most typical approach is to use grading or ranking. In these situations, the determination of the quality is less precise and more in the eye of the beholder.

Subjective and Objective Standards

When using the word "quality" in the sense of a derived property, we need to recognize that the determination of the quality of an entity can be based on both subjective and objective standards. When I first began to explore the question of the application of quality tools and techniques to technical disciplines, one of the first concepts I came upon was the distinction between the objective and the subjective nature of quality (11–16). While many quality practitioners argue that, for the quality of a good or service to have a sound foundation, it should be expressible in quantitative terms, many experts also recognize an intangible component that cannot be ignored. The objective and subjective perspectives correspond to so-called left-brain and right-brain thinking, respectively (17).

Much of the management training of the 1960s and 1970s was directed to quantification of information so that rational (objective) decisions could be made (18). The widespread introduction of personal computers into business life, coupled with a variety of software packages that made trade-off and what-if analyses relatively simple, reinforced the movement to numerically based decision making. A comprehensive study by Gambino and Gartenburg in 1979 summarized many of the approaches used in major industrial research and development organizations during the preceding 25 years to find ways to quantify the characteristics of a research and development program (19). As the amount of money spent on research and development grew to unprecedented levels, both industry and government managers sought techniques to measure what they were paying for. Even in this era, however, some managers recognized the difficulty in trying to put everything into quantitative terms. More recently, papers have started appearing on the importance of intuition in management decision making (20–23).

The question is not which approach to determining quality is correct. Rather, we need to recognize that both subjective and objective aspects are valid, and the challenge becomes understanding when and how to emphasize each of the two sides.

Objective Quality

Objective quality is based on quantitative measurements and is amenable to mathematical analysis. When a situation can be reduced to rational, quantitative, numerical terms, alternatives can be considered, consequences can be calculated, and the facts are available for all to consider and evaluate on the same terms. Mathematical analysis reduces ambiguity and is therefore vital and fundamental to many business decisions made in the context of contemporary U.S. economics. When working with the objective side of quality in a manufacturing environment, one must be competent in the science of metrology, understand the power and limitations of statistical analysis, and have tools available to help analyze large amounts of information.

The goal of research or development is to produce the most

accurate and precise information possible about a phenomenon, whereas the evaluation of the ultimate usefulness and effectiveness of the work is often speculative and subjective. New theories are evaluated by comparing the results of the predictions they engender with observed facts; the better the agreement, the more valid the theory is assumed to be. Much interesting technical work is derived from devising new experiments to test theories about events as yet unobserved. However, much of the scientific and technical work done today, especially in industry, is concerned with more immediate and concrete concerns; hence, the need for objective measures of accuracy and precision.

Subjective Quality

When we speak of the subjective nature of quality, we are discussing what is in the eye of the beholder. In objective quality, the conformance to standards usually can be determined numerically and often without the need for any human participation, while subjective quality, as we use the term, by definition cannot be measured by a machine. If a characteristic can be so measured, it automatically becomes part of the objective nature of the item. The closest thing to an exception to this is the summarization of survey or questionnaire data in numerical form. A potential trap is to view this as objective information, when in fact it is just a handy way of summarizing a mass of subjective information.

Related Terms

In this book, the term *quality control* is used in the classical sense of inspection of final or intermediate outputs. In the quality control field we see the importance of destructive and nondestructive testing. It is the field in which the science of metrology is widely used and in which statistical methods play a major role. It mainly involves the manufacturing world, but is beginning to include some portions of the service industries. It is the traditional role of quality professionals that began with the work of Shewhart (7).

Quality auditing is a means of evaluating the performance of all or part of a system to help assure that the products and processes are in conformance with the appropriate criteria, requirements, or standards. Audits commonly are conducted by independent groups to provide an unbiased evaluation of the situation. An audit may consider anything from the product itself to adherence to fundamental company policy.

Quality assurance is used as a synonym for management support in the preparation, execution, and evaluation activities. If you consider the functions performed by most quality assurance organizations, you will see that most, if not all, are activities performed to support management. While this is true of virtually all staff organizations, it seems to me to be particularly true of quality assurance organizations. The definitions given in the contemporary literature allude to this focus. Here, I am simply trying to reduce all the definitions to their simplest and most basic forms so that they will be applicable generally. Too often, the definitions have evolved around specific applications and that creates problems when they are applied in new areas.

References

1. J. M. Juran, ed., "China's Ancient History of Managing for Quality, Part I," *Quality Progress* 23(7):31–35 (July 1990).

2. D. R. Cox, "Quality and Reliability: Some Recent Developments and a Historical Perspective," *Journal of the Operational Research Society* 41(2):95–101 (1990).

3. David A. Garvin, *Managing Quality: The Strategic and Competitive Edge* (New York: Free Press, 1988), 3–20.

4. Robert F. Harper, ed., *The Code of Hammurabi: King of Babylon* (Chicago: University of Chicago Press, 1904).

5. M. M. Postan, E. E. Rich, and Edward Miller, eds., *The Cam-*

bridge Economic History of Europe, Vol. 3 (Cambridge, England: Cambridge University Press, 1965).

6. Lloyd P. Provost and Clifford L. Norman, "Variation through the Ages," *Quality Progress* 23(12):39–44 (December 1990).

7. W. A. Shewhart, *Economic Control of Quality of Manufactured Product* (New York: Van Nostrand, 1931).

8. J. M. Juran and Frank M. Gryna, Jr., *Quality Planning and Analysis: From Product Development through Use*, 2d ed. (New York: McGraw-Hill, 1980).

9. David A. Garvin, "What Does 'Product Quality' Really Mean?" *Sloan Management Review* 26(1):25–43 (Fall 1984).

10. International Organization for Standardization, *Quality— Vocabulary, International Standard ISO8402* (Geneva: International Organization for Standardization, June 15, 1986).

11. David Maister, *Professional Service Firm Management*, 3d ed. (Boston: Maister Associates, 1987), 41–43.

12. Robin L. Lawton, "Creating a Customer-Centered Culture in a Service Environment," *Annual Quality Congress Transactions/American Society for Quality Control, May 8–10, 1989* (Milwaukee, WI: American Society for Quality Control, 1989).

13. Michael B. Packer, "Measuring the Intangible in Productivity," *Technology Review* 86(2):48–57 (February/March 1983).

14. "The Balance of Quality," editorial, *Quality Progress* 16(10):6 (October 1983).

15. Jack R. Meredith and Samuel J. Mantel, Jr., *Project Management: A Managerial Approach* (New York: John Wiley, 1985), 55.

16. *The New Encyclopedia Britannica*, 15th ed. (Chicago: Encyclopædia Britannica, 1982), "Aesthetics."

17. Betty Edwards, *Drawing on the Right Side of the Brain* (Los Angeles: Tarcher, 1979).

18. Charles H. Kepner and Benjamin B. Tregoe, *The New Rational Manager* (Princeton, NJ: Kepner-Tregoe, 1981).

19. Anthony J. Gambino and Morris Gartenberg, *Industrial R&D Management* (New York: National Association of Accountants, 1979).

20. Weston H. Agor, "How Top Executives Use Their Intuition to Make Important Decisions," *Business Horizons* 29(1): 39–43 (January–February 1986).

21. Frank H. Squires, "Management by Viscera," *Quality* 29(5): 74 (May 1990).

22. Terry Lynn Payne, "A Decision Model which Considers Qualitative Factors," *International Journal of Technology Management* 4(1):1–7 (1989).

23. Daniel Isenberg, "How Senior Managers Think," *Computerworld* 18(50):23–44 (December 10, 1984).

Chapter 3

The Place of Research and Development in Industry

At this point, there is a need to define a few additional terms as they are used in this book. First, it is important to discriminate between *research* and *development*. I believe some of the difficulty experienced in trying to apply quality principles to these activities comes from treating them as one field, R&D, rather than as two separate and distinct fields. The definitions given next, which are adapted in part from various reference works, point out some of these differences (1–3). The differences become significant when we discuss the means of evaluating the outputs of the two functions.

Research usually is considered to be studious inquiry or examination, especially investigation or experimentation aimed at the discovery and interpretation of facts or the revision of accepted theories or laws in the light of new facts. Research often is divided into two categories: basic and applied. The difference between the two depends on the ultimate use for the information (product) derived from the research process. If the information is being generated for its own sake and the people interested are limited to the immediate scientific com-

27

munity, the research is considered basic. If, on the other hand, there is a potential product in mind, and the ultimate users will be consumers, then the research is considered applied. For example, basic research currently is being done in the field of high-energy physics. Much of the work is experimental and has the goal of expanding our understanding of the fundamental nature of matter. Although this understanding ultimately might help us produce better materials, the immediate interest is intellectual and there are no products in mind. In contrast, current research in molecular chemistry often is oriented toward the ultimate, specific goal of creating new plastics for well-defined applications. Research in technical fields usually is done by people with advanced degrees, often doctorates, in such fields as chemistry, physics, biology, or mathematics. A smaller amount of research is done by individuals with engineering degrees in such fields as fluid mechanics, electronics, or materials science.

Development is the conversion of scientific information into such things as hardware, materials, or rules of procedure. The output of the development process is technology. One of the more interesting development programs in recent years was the part of the space program that involved development of various kite and glider concepts for the recovery of capsules as they returned from space. The basic scientific information on the aerodynamics of these concepts was established and a development program was needed to translate this information into useful, reliable hardware. Development work commonly is done by both scientists and engineers, that is, people who have degrees either in one of the sciences or in one of the engineering disciplines.

Science means knowledge covering general truths or the operation of general laws, especially as obtained and tested through scientific methods (4). Science is the product of the research process. *Scientific information*, as used here, is a synonym for science. Scientific information takes many forms, ranging from the basic laws of nature to correlations of experimental data, and includes theories ranging from the Big Bang to Darwin's theory of evolution. The scope of information encompasses concepts as varied as Newton's laws of motion and the explanation of how the pyramids of Egypt were constructed. The word *science* also is applied commonly to a wide variety of disciplines that are characterized by the possibility of making precise statements susceptible to some sort of check or proof. In this sense, the field of quality is on the verge of becoming a science (5).

Technology designates the items, materials, tools, techniques, or rules of procedure that are produced by the development process. Technology helps form the bridge between scientific information and commercial products (6). For a quality control organization, a set of gauge blocks and the proper techniques for using them would constitute a part of the technology needed to fulfill the organization's mission.

In most scientific and engineering schools, the majority of the material taught is science. Science tends to stay fairly constant so textbooks can be written that will stay correct for several years. New advances in science are found in technical papers and learned journals. Eventually, these advances will become accepted and also find their way into textbooks. While the sources of technological information overlap those of scientific information to some extent, the more common sources of technology are handbooks, manufacturers' catalogs, and industrial codes and standards.

From Idea to Product

From the above definitions, it can be seen that a pattern of processes and products is emerging. Figure 3.1 shows how this pattern continues for the evolution of an idea into a commercially manufactured product. The basic pattern has many possible variations and additional refinements; however, for the sake of simplicity and brevity, only the fundamental phases are discussed in detail here. For situations in which the science and technology already exist, the research and development steps are not necessary. In much of the commercial world, this is the case and a manufacturer simply has to put information that already exists into practice. The government has large programs

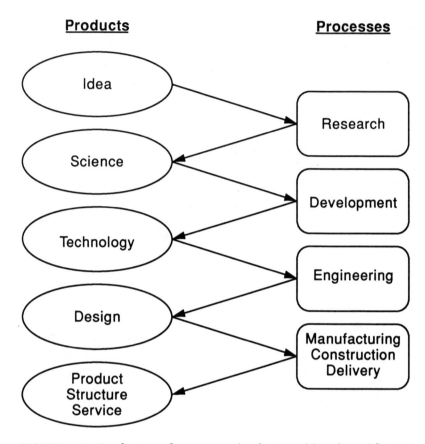

FIGURE 3.1. Products and processes in the transition from idea to implementation.

in place to transfer the science and technology developed at taxpayers' expense in the defense, energy, and space programs into commercial products. When the technology is complex, there are often one or more intermediate steps, referred to as pilot plant or prototype phases. There are also situations in which there are several phases of engineering interspersed among the other activities.

The same basic pattern exists whether the outcome is to be a single product, such as the construction of an office building, or multiple products, such as the mass production of washing machines. In the case of single-output activities, one simply could substitute the term "construction" for "manufacturing." Project-management specialists have developed tools and techniques to help manage such activities (7,8). Regardless of whether a single item, such as a building, or multiple items, such as washing machines, are being produced, the basic stages from conception of the idea to the embodiment of that idea in a product are essentially the same. The "products" created during these different stages are judged according to different standards or requirements depending on their location in the life cycle of the product or project.

Life Cycles

In order to help clarify some of the aspects of the research and development processes, it is helpful to see where these activities fit into the product or project life cycle. Most approaches to defining life cycles show the object or activity under consideration going through the stages of birth, growth, maturity, decline, and death. Product life cycles usually are associated with just the marketing phase of an item and begin with the introduction of the product into the marketplace. In reality, products, like biological organisms, have a life cycle that begins at conception and in which birth is really a midpoint in their temporal journey. We take this more comprehensive view and start with the conception of the product and carry the analysis to the point of death or rebirth.

This complete life cycle is shown as the abscissa of Fig. 3.2. The research and development phases occur in the prenatal period just after conception and hence are critical to the development of the entity. While the life cycle could be subdivided into finer stages or classified somewhat differently, the subdivisions used here suffice for the purpose of this discussion (9,10). Some reflection reveals a striking similarity to the biological case. Small changes at this stage can have profound effects on the future life of the organism (product). Just as prenatal care is critical in the nurturing of biological offspring, so prenatal at-

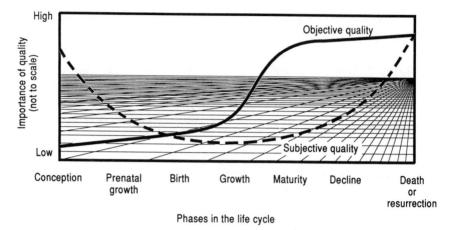

FIGURE 3.2. Objective and subjective aspects of quality vary over the life cycle.

tention is of major importance in the life of a product. In the same fashion, the effect of a small perturbation generally will not show up for a long period of time, often many years in the case of complex technical hardware in which quality is of the most importance.

In industrial situations, it is desirable to see and evaluate immediately the impact of small changes in each variable on all stages of the life cycle of the system. Unfortunately, most real systems are much too complex for this type of analysis, and actual outcomes do not become apparent until far in the future. Nevertheless, we usually can assume safely that the application of quality principles at the research and development stages in a product's life will increase the probability of a successful outcome in the marketplace.

Once an item is in production, if a new machine is purchased (for example), the rate of production will change by a certain amount, the cost of producing the item will vary by so much, and the dimensions of the item can be held to tighter limits. This type of analysis is not possible in the early stages of the life cycle.

Objective and subjective considerations. The ordinate of Fig. 3.2 shows how the importance of the objective and subjective aspects of quality vary over the life cycle of an item. The solid line represents objective quality and the dashed line subjective quality. Obviously, the details are imprecise and there are exceptions to any such generalization. Nevertheless, I believe the basic concept is valid and provides a helpful frame of reference for discussion.

At the point of conception, the evaluation of a new idea for an object or service is based largely on subjective opinions and intuitive judgments. Assuming the idea is accepted by a company's management, the product begins its life with the appropriate research, development, and engineering phases. As the amount of quantitative information at each stage increases, the evaluation of the product at that stage can begin to be made on more objective grounds. An entrepreneur would like all the information to be as quantitative as possible from the very beginning since that should reduce the risk in deciding whether or not to go on to the next stage. Unfortunately, this is not possible and such decisions generally are made with a large subjective component that diminishes as the life cycle progresses.

We must be careful to distinguish between the science or technology being considered and the embodiment of that information in a commercial product. There are numerous references in the literature describing methods for evaluating the ultimate commercial success of research proposals (11,12). The goal of these evaluation methods is to bring much desired, and frequently quite helpful, quantitative information to bear on the subject. The fact remains that the majority of the information available on which to evaluate the ultimate commercial success of a concept is still basically subjective during the early stages of the concept's life. It is not until the product based on the concept actually enters the marketplace that objective measures can be developed regarding the cost and income associated with the product. In this book, the science and technology are considered for their own sakes and the evaluation of commercial potential is left to the experts in that field.

Once a product or service is introduced into the market-place, the classical quality tools can be very useful in keeping track of the consistency of conformance to standards, in identifying opportunities for improving the products or the processes used to produce them, and in correcting problems that have arisen. Indeed, the common quality tools described by such practitioners as those whose work appears in Refs. 13 and 14 (and whose works are based on the earlier teachings of Deming, Juran, Shewhart, and other pioneers) were developed for this part of the life cycle and are most useful there. When a mass-produced product reaches its mature phase, the quality of the product should be amenable to quantitative evaluation. There will be a stable base of information on the characteristics of the items produced that forms the basis for comparison of potential improvements. During the start-up phase of a new system when this stability has not been established yet, it is often difficult to determine whether improvements in quality of the product are brought about by small, deliberate changes in the process or whether they are the natural result of the growth and learning processes. Once again using the biological analogy, the growth phase is very similar to the changes that occur in humans during adolescence; it is difficult to distinguish improvements that occur naturally from those that are brought about by education and training.

Juran and Gryna discuss two situations in which there are opportunities for improvement in the quality of a product or service (15). These opportunities come about because of what Juran and Gryna call *chronic problems* and *sporadic problems*. For these concepts to be useful, there must be a suitable, stable base case against which comparisons can be made. In the pre-natal phases of a product's life cycle, there is no base case to use as a reference. In technical work, the best that one can hope for is a few data points that can be compared to a theoretical prediction. If the data agree with the theory, one has some confidence that an extrapolation to the next level of complexity and sophistication is justified. If, on the other hand, they do not agree, one must evaluate both the data and the theory to see if either or both require additional refinement. This condition is especially true in the construction and fabrication areas. One produces a design, and from it generates a cost estimate (one data point). Ideas for improvements are, at best, projections of how the cost might be reduced or the performance improved if certain changes are made to the baseline design, but there are no concrete data on which to base the projections.

Finally, at the end of its life cycle, every entity—animate or inanimate—will die and be reborn in some manner. In the case of commercial products, the death will come about because the item either has lost its usefulness or has been replaced by another product. At this stage, the decision to let the product die or to attempt to resurrect it in some modified form frequently is made on the basis of criteria that are largely subjective. Although some quantitative data may be available on costs and market potential, the uncertainties are large enough to force the decision to be made on the basis of judgments and expectations rather than hard facts.

Feasibility considerations. Another perspective for viewing the initial phases of the product life cycle is to consider that, in the interval between conception and birth, one is attempting to verify various aspects of the feasibility of the product or service. There are essentially five types of feasibility: scientific, technical, engineering, economic, and commercial. Figure 3.3 shows the feasibilities mapped onto the product life cycle.

Studies of scientific feasibility are designed to determine whether the idea is scientifically valid. Quite often this phase is done on paper with little or no experimental data. Any experimental work that is done will be on a lab scale and will be designed to verify such things as physical properties. Equipment will be small and often will consist of standard laboratory items. Physical and temporal constants will be significantly different from those proposed in the ultimate configuration. The primary types of questions to be asked are: Does the concept obey known scientific laws? Are there any fatal flaws in the logic? Does the concept require materials that, in principle, cannot be produced? The scientific information must serve to answer these questions.

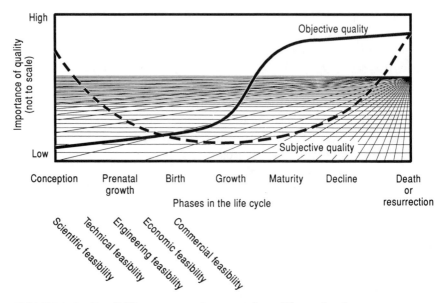

FIGURE 3.3. Feasibility types as they pertain to life cycle phases.

The development phase is concerned with technical feasibility. Here, the concern is that the basic elements of materials, equipment, and techniques be available. To determine the technical feasibility, it is often necessary to model the system under consideration physically and show how all the components interact with one another. If the process is designed to produce a material, that material must be produced and it must be produced in the manner proposed. Equipment sizes again probably will be out of proportion to the ultimate commercial scale and will be selected from regularly available items adapted to suit the circumstances.

The next phase evaluates what commonly is called engineering feasibility. In this step, the question is whether the elements required can be assembled into practical systems. Any experimental work done to verify the engineering feasibility generally is done at the pilot plant scale; a small version of the system is fabricated and the key components are modeled.

Once the engineering feasibility is established, the evaluation moves from a mainly technical perspective to an economic one. The information developed from the engineering feasibility evaluation is coupled with information on labor and material costs to determine the economic feasibility. In the final step, all the information is tied together with a market analysis to provide the commercial feasibility.

Although the researchers and developers are involved mostly in the first two steps, an understanding of the other aspects is helpful in putting their efforts into perspective. (It also can be of great value in selling research or development programs to managers if the entire spectrum of concerns can be addressed.) The information generated in the research and development phases of a program is important for two reasons. First, it provides the basis on which the decision whether to continue the program or not will be made. Inadequate or incorrect information could cause a potentially profitable program to be canceled prematurely. One of the most important examples of this was the failure of the German scientific community working on the atomic bomb in World War II to pursue the use of graphite as a moderator for atomic piles because the scientific information from the German laboratories on the properties of graphite was incorrect (16). Second, this information will determine many of the key parameters for the product as well as the process to produce the product. If the information is inaccurate, major errors could be made in such areas as the sizing of equipment or the requirements for energy. Recognizing the potential impact research and development work can have on the future of a company should lend additional weight to the need for producing accurate reliable science and technology during the research and development phases of a program. Figure 3.4 shows the relationship between the percentage of resources committed and the percentage of resources actually expended as a project moves from research to production.

Even more important, perhaps, is the fact that in basic research, the scientific community relies on the validity of existing work to guide the future of the discipline. Thus, while there might not be a direct impact on a particular company, an entire field can be misguided because of incorrect research results.

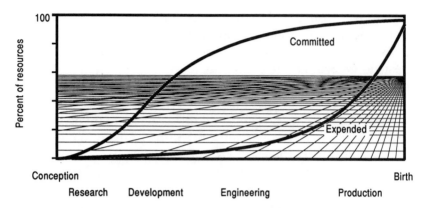

FIGURE 3.4. Resources committed and resources expended on a product as it goes from research to production.

Comparison with Other Industrial Activities

Now that we have seen where research and development activities fit into the product life cycle and have examined some of the characteristics of these activities, let us see how they compare with typical industrial activities. Figure 3.5 depicts some typical industrial activities in terms of the amount of repetition of the product and the tangibility of that product.

The upper right quadrant of Fig. 3.5 represents the area of classical manufacturing, in which many units are produced and their tangibility is high. In this region, the concepts of quality, quality control, and quality assurance had their origin and are most used and best developed. It was in this type of activity that W. A. Shewhart originated the concept of statistical quality control (17). When many units are being produced, it is possible to attempt to make each unit, or at least each batch of units, better than the last. It is also possible to develop good information on the variation of quality with cost and time. Industrial engineering, especially that branch dealing with time and motion study, is very useful in quantifying the requirements for personnel, equipment, and procedures for this type of activity. It is in this area that statistical tools are very useful and the concept of continuous improvement can have its best application.

This area tends to be the most quantitative in nature. Here, the cost of a quality program generally will be more than offset by the savings it creates by reducing scrap and rework; these savings lead to the concept that "Quality Is Free" (18). Decisions about tool replacement can be made on solid ground; the cost and productive capacity of a new machine can be measured against the maintenance charges of the machine being considered for replacement and an objective decision reached on the basis of the costs and benefits of the various alternatives under consideration.

The lower right quadrant represents the construction and fabrication industries. In this area, the product is again very tangible but the number of repetitions is low; often there is only a single case. Statistical methods are not useful except for some of the secondary operations that are repetitive. The danger is to overlook the forest for the trees; the goal is not to keep track of how many drawing changes were made, but how well the plant worked. In this domain, the quality principle of doing it right the first time is paramount. Some of the key variables are time (schedule) and money (budget). These become important quali-

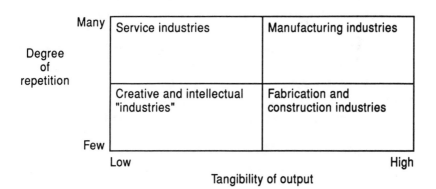

FIGURE 3.5. Industry types classified by degrees of repetition and tangibility.

ty indicators in the construction and fabrication fields and cannot be ignored.

In a manufacturing environment, while minimization of scrap during setup is important and should not be overlooked, the amount of materials consumed during the setup phase is usually small and there is a trade-off between planning for zero scrap during setup and the value of the scrap. This is not the case in construction and fabrication projects. Once a construction or fabrication job is complete, there are no more units over which to spread the cost of errors. Therefore, it is more important to do adequate planning and preparation before the job is started. There is an analogy to the just-in-time philosophy of the factory and that is to have the appropriate materials on site at the correct time. If the materials arrive too early, they can get lost or stolen, or deteriorate; if they arrive too late, the entire project is delayed. It is this situation that has led to the development of the project-management concept.

The upper left quadrant of Fig. 3.5 is the domain of the service industry. In this region, although the repetitions are many, the outcome is less tangible. This is an area of major interest to the quality profession today. As the world moves to a more service-oriented environment, it becomes increasingly important to be able to define and evaluate the quality of the service being provided and received. The main difficulty lies in the fact that the evaluation of the product is in the eye of the receiver. The customer may always be right, but if you do not know what the customer wants or how he or she is going to evaluate you, it is hard to design a system that will deliver the right kind of service. Statistics can be useful here, once the appropriate measures are defined. Again, the trap can be counting the number of customers served rather than the quality of the service provided.

One of the more useful tools is the customer survey in which receivers are asked to rate the service on a numerical scale. The field of surveying people and interpreting the results is developing rapidly and is becoming more helpful all the time.

Finally, the lower left quadrant of Fig. 3.5 is of primary interest to us for it is in these industries that research and development work is accomplished. This is the province of creative work; it is where such activities as art and literature and musical composition take place. The area is of interest not only to the quality profession but also to the management profession (19,20). The type of work done in this sector generally is done only once, or at most a few times, and the evaluation of it is largely subjective, at least initially. In very basic research, the final determination of the correctness of the work is often years or decades in the future. Another interesting feature of this type of work is that the best people to evaluate a piece of work are frequently outside the organization that is doing the work.

The application of quality principles to this area, especially to research and development, is still in the formative stage. So far, the main thrusts have been to seek out aspects that are amenable to quantification and documentation, such as the number of documents produced, calibration of instruments, and standardization of procedures. George W. Roberts' book, *Quality Assurance in Research and Development*, focuses on such activities as design control, control of purchased material, and control of measuring and test equipment (21). A Department of Energy study on the development of alternatives to conventional spark ignition engines used a quality program to control documentation, procurement, material identification, material handling and storage, and inspections (22). In an article in *Research Management* that summarized a workshop on the relationship between quality assurance and research and development, the author noted that "all of these [programs and studies] represent the beginnings of a widespread effort to look at the quality of R&D in some quantifiable way in order to determine what can be done to improve it" and concluded that it was "easy to say, tough to do" (23, p. 11). In Chapter 5, a comprehensive approach to putting quality to work in the research and development environment is described. The approach will not only help when there is quantifiable information with which to work, but also will help deal with the subjective aspects of the field. It provides the basis for setting up a procedure that covers all parts of a quality program, from inception through evaluation to final documentation.

References

1. Richard Leifer and Thomas Triscari, Jr., "Research versus Development: Differences and Similarities," *IEEE Transactions on Engineering Management* EM-34(2):71–78 (May 1987).

2. Carl Heyel, ed., *The Encyclopedia of Management* (New York: Reinhold, 1963), "Basic Research: Management Aspects."

3. Russell F. Moore, ed., *AMA Management Handbook* (New York: American Management Association, 1970), pp. 7.1–7.3.

4. Tyrus Hillway, *Introduction to Research* (Boston: Houghton Mifflin, 1956), pp. 11–13.

5. *Encyclopedia of Science and Technology*, 6th ed. (New York: McGraw-Hill, 1987), "Scientific Methods."

6. *Encyclopedia of Science and Technology*, 6th ed. (New York: McGraw-Hill, 1987), "Technology."

7. Thomas A. DeCotiis and Lee Dyer, "Defining and Measuring Project Performance," in *Project Management: Selected Papers from* Research Management *during the Period 1977–1984* (New York: Industrial Research Institute, 1985), 23–28.

8. Jack R. Meredith and Samuel J. Mantel, Jr., *Project Management, a Managerial Approach* (New York: John Wiley, 1985).

9. Richard A. Pappas and Donald S. Remer, "Measuring R&D Productivity," *Research Management* 28(3):89–96 (May–June 1985).

10. John R. Dixon and Michael R. Duffey, "The Neglect of Engineering Design," *California Management Review* 32(2):9–23 (Winter 1990).

11. William J. Spencer, "Research to Product: A Major U.S.

Challenge," *California Management Review* 32(2):45–53 (Winter 1990).

12. Ashok K. Gupta and David L. Wilemon, "Accelerating the Development of Technology-Based New Products," *California Management Review* 32(2):24–44 (Winter 1990).

13. Kaoru Ishikawa, *Guide to Quality Control* (White Plains, NY: Quality Resources, 1976).

14. Shigeru Mizuno, ed., *Management for Quality Improvement: The Seven New QC Tools* (Cambridge, MA: Productivity Press, 1988).

15. J. M. Juran and Frank M. Gryna, Jr., *Quality Planning and Analysis from Product Development through Use*, 2d ed. (New York: McGraw-Hill, 1980).

16. Richard Rhodes, *The Making of the Atomic Bomb* (New York: Simon and Schuster, 1986).

17. W. A. Shewhart, *Economic Control of Quality of Manufactured Product* (New York: Van Nostrand, 1931).

18. Philip B. Crosby, *Quality Is Free: The Art of Making Quality Certain* (New York: McGraw-Hill, 1979).

19. Bradford L. Berglind and Charles D. Scales, "White-Collar Productivity: Seeing through the Camouflage," *Management Review* 76(6):41–46 (June 1987).

20. Robert S. Root-Bernstein, "Strategies of Research," *Research Technology Management* 32(3):36–41 (May–June 1989).

21. George W. Roberts, *Quality Assurance in Research and Development* (New York: Marcel Dekker, 1983).

22. H. Bankaitis, "Reliability and Quality Assurance in Research and Development," *Quality Progress* 17(3):10–15 (March 1984).

23. Michael F. Wolff, "Quality/Process Control: What R&D Can Do," *Research Management* 29(1):9–11 (January–February 1986).

Benefits and Costs of a Quality Program

One of the most common criteria for the success or failure of a product is whether it made a profit in the marketplace. Money is an easy parameter to measure (in principle, at least) and is important in practically all endeavors. In a manufacturing environment, it is relatively easy to calculate the impact of new or improved methods or materials on the cost of an item and the benefits usually are measurable within fairly short periods of time. In research and development, on the other hand, a difficulty often is encountered in attempting to assign monetary value to research and development results in that the impact of those results on the marketplace may be far in the future. In addition, once a new product has entered the marketplace, many other factors that have come into play since the time the technical work was completed also will influence the product's success or failure. Fortunately, money is not the only parameter that can be used to evaluate costs and benefits. In this chapter, we examine some perspectives for assessing the costs and benefits of a quality program in a technical organization.

An Analogy from Mathematics

The difference in our ability to predict the consequences of changes in inputs or processes on the outputs of manufacturing and the outputs of research and development is similar to the difference between boundary-value and initial-value problems in the branch of mathematics dealing with the solution of differential equations. In a boundary-value problem, the conditions of interest are specified at all the boundaries—both geometric and temporal—of the domain of interest. The solution to the differential equation governing the situation then must satisfy these conditions. If changes are made in the boundary conditions, the equations must be solved again to satisfy the new conditions. An analogous situation in the manufacturing world would be the replacement of one machine with another on an assembly line. In this case, the current production rates, maintenance costs, and similar factors are known, and the future conditions in terms of replacement costs, expected production rates, and reduced maintenance costs can be well described. With this information available, a manager can calculate fairly accurately what effect the new machine will have on costs, production rates, tolerances, maintenance requirements, and other significant factors. Some uncertainty will exist, but assuming adequate study is made, the predictions of costs and other factors will be reasonably correct.

In initial-value problems, on the other hand, certain conditions of interest are specified only at one boundary and the solution of the differential equation will determine the conditions at the other boundaries. Many initial-value problems encountered in science and engineering involve nonlinear partial differential equations. Quite often, the equations are so complex that analytical solutions cannot be obtained and recourse must be made to numerical methods using high-speed electronic computers. Solutions to this type of problem, whether obtained analytically or numerically, are often extremely sensitive to the initial conditions, and small changes in those conditions can affect the shape of the solution dramatically. Most research and development tasks are analogous to initial-value problems.

At the start of a research or development project, the workers know where they are and how to get started, but the future course of events is uncertain and small changes in approach or assumptions can alter that course radically.

Because of these uncertainties, the prediction of future benefits and costs from a quality program in a technical organization cannot be as reliable or precise as those made in situations in which there is more experience and precedent. When a scientific discovery has reached the point of utilization in an industrial product, the financial benefits generally far outweigh the original costs. However, the benefits and costs still are hard to define. For example, what should be included in the cost of the research and development that led to the advent of the personal computer? Do you include some or all costs associated with computer development in general, or do you include some fraction? The accounting of the obvious and not so obvious costs represents a challenge few would undertake. Similarly, what are the benefits? Should the benefits include profits for computer manufacturers, time saved by organizations using the computers, and even lives saved by improved medical diagnostics? The possibilities are numerous and philosophically interesting, but they are not much quantitative help to managers or entrepreneurs.

Trade-offs

When considering the impact of a quality program on a research or development organization or any organization in which only one, or at most a few, items are created, one is trading the costs of more formalized planning, record keeping, and adherence to procedures for the potential benefits of making fewer mistakes, going down fewer blind alleys and reducing the number of unforeseen results. Because it is never possible to know how many mistakes would have been made if the planning for a project had not been done, it is never possible to quantify the time, money, and effort saved by planning. At best, one can estimate the potential difficulties and then use judgment to allocate a reasonable amount of effort for preparations that will avoid the known problems. At the current stage of sophistication in the quality profession, I do not believe it is possible to tell whether a quality program will be free of costs in a research and development environment. The problem is that in any situation in which there is a single output, there is no valid basis for comparison.

The cost of quality or the cost of an improvement can be treated as an initial-value problem because the future condition does not exist yet. Without concrete knowledge of this future condition, no valid basis for comparison exists—only a predicted value exists. Consider a situation in which a company uncovers a potential market for a new type of gas compressor to handle hazardous materials associated with a waste management operation. Three options might be available to the company. The first option simply involves using existing technologies slightly modified to suit the new conditions. An example could be taking an existing compressor and plating the components to extend their lives in the more corrosive environment. In this case, the costs can be predicted fairly accurately and can serve as a base case. Questions may be asked about the market size and perhaps about reliability, but these can be handled by allowing some variation in the assumptions. For the second option, assume someone in the development laboratory proposes making the entire compressor out of a material that will be more resistant to the environment, but has never been used in this type of application. The potential benefits might include lower maintenance costs and less leakage, real benefits when dealing with hazardous materials. With this scenario, estimates have to be made not only of the production costs, but of the cost to develop the new machine. The third option is even more interesting (but also more uncertain): the research laboratory proposes working on an entirely new material that should be virtually corrosion resistant in the new environment and inexpensive to produce, but perhaps more expensive to fabricate. There are many references in the management literature that give advice on how to select projects and manage such situations, but often the conclusion is to trust one's intuition, based on knowledge of the track record of the research and development people involved and an assessment of the technical and economic uncertainties.

In the next section, we examine the benefits and costs of a quality program for research and development organizations only. Ideally, an entire company will participate in a quality program, and some improvements in purchasing, maintenance, and other departments will benefit research and development personnel also. However, the benefits to the research and development department and its members are significant enough to warrant putting a program in place in the technical department regardless of whether or not the rest of the company has seen the light.

We consider only the near-term benefits and costs. Our focus is on the technical work per se and not its ultimate embodiment in some commercial product. In the translation from scientific information to commercial entity, too many intermediate factors exist that can influence the success of the product in the marketplace; for instance, the collapse of a bridge in a violent wind storm is not a reason to question the validity of the basic laws of mechanics. For our purposes, we must be careful to sort out the concerns surrounding the research and development work from its ultimate use as some product or service.

Naturally, for a company funding research and development, the value of the information produced by those departments in the market is a major consideration and should be considered in the company's planning and evaluation. Although the details of such calculations are beyond the scope of this book, an appreciation of the impact of the quality of research and development outputs on a company's success can provide an extremely useful perspective to the people doing the research and development work.

The Benefits of a Quality Program

As we consider benefit and cost analyses for research and development functions, we should note that the analyses do not produce hard and fast, numerical, objective results. However, they provide useful perspectives about the work. We look at the question from five points of view, those of the person doing the work, the department of which the worker is a part, the company (which could be a commercial company, a university, or a government agency), the technical community involved, and the public. Each of these entities derives some benefit from the task, and it costs each entity something. We look at all the benefits first and then examine the costs.

Benefits to the worker. Most of us are very familiar with WII-FM (What's in it for me?). If a quality program is going to be successful, the users of the program must see some real benefit for themselves, or they simply will treat the program as if it were a management fad. For the knowledge workers, who already have significant control over the details of their work, the benefits will be less observable than for assembly-line workers, who often receive more opportunity for participation in the planning and execution of their work as a result of the institution of a quality program. I suspect quality programs that fail in manufacturing organizations do so because the workers cannot see any significant benefit. If some portion of the profits and other benefits derived from a quality program are not channeled to the workers, they will remain disinterested participants.

The primary benefits to the knowledge worker are improvement in the understanding of their assignments and responsibilities. Once a quality program is in place in a knowledge-based organization, one change that takes place subtly is the realization that many things that were being done without much thought now are being done deliberately. The people involved have a reason, and a good one at that, for doing what they are doing. Upon reflection, one realizes that a logical, well-defined, deliberately executed program is the basis of all effective technical work. Good experimental work is well planned and thought out ahead of time. One of the best experimentalists I have known explained that he regularly began his experimental programs by drafting the final report. This process brought the requirements into clear focus and showed the specific steps needed to achieve the required finished product.

In addition to these first-order benefits, technical people

usually find they are receiving greater personal satisfaction from doing their work in a way that provides them assurance of success for their work. Workers also find their job security enhanced. The skills they learn as part of the quality program not only improve their ability to perform their present assignments, but also prepare them for other assignments in their present organization or (should the need arise) in a new one. A final benefit is the possibility of personal recognition and monetary reward. As the advantages of quality programs in research and development become more apparent to companies, one can expect the recognition and reward programs familiar in manufacturing to become instituted in the technical organizations also.

Benefits to the technical staff. The benefits of a quality program to the technical staff occur because the efforts of the individuals are focused on meaningful, well-understood programs. A vital synergism appears from having the members of a knowledge-based organization understand that all the members are contributing to a common goal even if they are working on completely different tasks. Morale improves also when group members begin to support and encourage one another and when productive formal evaluation replaces informal, often inaccurate and incomplete, personal assessments of co-workers' contributions.

Benefits to the company. The company (and any external agency) sponsoring the research and development benefit in two ways from a quality program. First, it now has greater confidence that its resources are being well managed. From the company's perspective, timing is still a major consideration and the economic benefits will not be determined until sometime in the future. However, in the near term, the technical staff will become more aware of the impact of their work and they will be able to see how their efforts fit into the long-range goals of the company. The second benefit is that, in an increasingly litigious world, a suitable quality program will provide considerable evidence, should the need arise, of solid planning, execution, and evaluation of the technical portion of a program.

Benefits to the technical community. Next to the individual research or development practitioner, the technical community is the greatest beneficiary of a quality program. The growth of science and technology depends on sound interpretations of reliable information. As science and technology become more complex and the gathering of new data becomes more expensive, the cost of traveling wrong roads becomes unduly costly. Although a quality program cannot guarantee that miracles will occur at specified junctures in a program, it can help minimize the number of errors introduced into a program and provide a structured framework for evaluating the results.

One criticism leveled against instituting quality activities, especially those involving evaluations, into research, development, or any other knowledge enterprise is that a quality program will stifle creativity. However, the knowledge worker is the primary evaluator of his or her work. An artist will not place a piece of art on exhibit or put it up for sale if it does not satisfy the artist's own standards. Outside critics voice their opinions, and the buying public provides evaluations, but, ultimately, the artist decides whether the work conforms to his or her standards. The same is true for the technical worker. Until the worker is satisfied with the results, the work probably will not be published. Just as quality awareness can help artists understand their personal standards and the criteria of their potential customers, it also can help researchers understand their personal requirements for the work they publish and the needs of the development workers who will use their results. A quality awareness can avoid the ivory-tower syndrome, in which a worker spends an inappropriate amount of time developing a comprehensive understanding of a situation when all that was needed was a simple yes or no answer. Conversely, an awareness of quality can eliminate sketchy answers provided for problems for which more detail or more accurate values are needed.

Benefits to society. The members of society ultimately use the results of research and development work and they also must live with the consequences of bad judgments and with the costs of incorrect work. Recalling the illustration (Fig. 3.4) showing how costs of products are affected by information and decisions made at research and development stages in the product life cycle, it is clear that any and all efforts to improve the quality of information at these early stages can provide significant cost avoidances to society. Science and technology have been dominant factors in determining our present standard of living. A sound quality program, properly directed, can enhance further the future impact of science and technology on our society, both financially and environmentally.

The Costs of a Quality Program

The costs of any overhead program can be broken down into two rather broad categories: (1) the direct monetary costs of the staff involved in administering the program, and (2) the indirect costs that result from the interaction of the staff with the producers. We will not dwell at length on the direct costs of the staff, but will concentrate on the costs to the same five groups for which benefits were identified above: the worker, the technical staff, the company, the technical community, and society.

Costs to the worker. For the worker, the principal cost is in time taken away from the worker's primary interest. Most of the technical people I know consider time they do not spend on their technical assignments as time lost. Many will explain that ideas come from a certain amount of thinking and doing, and worrying about other concerns takes away from the task at hand. The majority recognize that they have a responsibility to their employers and are willing to accept what they consider a reasonable amount of administrative burden, provided the reason for the work is made clear and held to a minimum. To put it another way, a researcher's standards for a quality program are that it be understandable, have reasonable requirements, and cause minimal impact on the technical work. These standards can be met easily by providing superior orientation, designing the program on a rational model such as that proposed in this book, and providing ample administrative support in such areas as planning, record keeping, and reporting.

Costs to the technical staff. There should be no additional costs to the technical staff from an appropriate quality program, other than the aggregated costs to the individual members. Having a quality program in operation in a technical organization should not create a situation in which the whole is greater than the sum of the parts. The potential problem is that an inappropriate quality program will be imposed. If this happens, morale and productivity can be reduced by amounts disproportionate to the time demanded by the quality program.

Costs to the company. The costs to the company and any outside agency are twofold. First, there are direct costs attributable to maintaining a staff of quality professionals to perform the training, documentation, evaluation, and record keeping. The second costs to the company come from loss of output from the technical staff; this loss of output also has two components. One component is the time actually spent on such quality activities as attending training sessions, preparing additional documentation required by the quality program, and participating in evaluations. The second component is the time lost because of inefficiencies in the quality program; there should be no losses in this second class. Given an effective program that is well prepared and executed, I firmly believe these costs eventually will approach zero. However, there will be some inefficiencies and, therefore, time lost at the start of any new program. These costs must be considered when inaugurating any quality program.

Costs to the technical community. Like the technical staff, the technical community should not incur costs other than the accumulated loss of productivity from time spent on quality matters instead of technical work. If, however, an inappropriate quality program is imposed on several organizations the employees of which all are members of the same technical community, additional costs can occur. This situation can arise when a government agency or a standard-setting body imposes inappropriate requirements on a class of organizations. When this happens, there is a strong probability that additional costs will occur, not only from the loss in productivity, but also from time spent by the members of the community attempting to eliminate, or at least modify, the requirements.

Costs to society. Because society ultimately receives the benefits of science and technology, society also bears the burden of the costs of the quality program that accompanied the generation of the science and technology. The direct financial costs of a quality program should be a small percentage of the total cost (or price) of the final goods or services. Research and development costs average less than 5% of the total cost of an item. A comprehensive quality program should involve no more than one full-time-equivalent (FTE) person for each group of 20 FTE staff members, or approximately a 5% impact. Consequently, the total impact on the cost of the item will be less than 0.3%. If nothing else, this cost can be considered a low-cost insurance policy.

The Bottom Line

There is no doubt in my mind that an effective quality program can be of benefit to any research or development organization. I also am convinced that the observable costs can be minimal—less than 5% of the operating budget of the organization. However, as the discussion above shows, no satisfactory way exists to quantify either the total benefits or costs in economic terms. As a result, both managers and members of the technical staff are frequently uneasy about adopting a quality program for their organizations. Because many of the benefits and costs can be observed and described only in subjective terms, the decision to start and continue a quality program must rest as much on intuition, trust, and faith as on anything else.

By building the quality program from concepts familiar to and accepted by the technical community, the probability of acceptance should be enhanced significantly. The remainder of this book seeks to increase the likelihood of acceptance by the research and development staff by using terminology and techniques derived from concepts already familiar to the majority of people with scientific or engineering backgrounds.

Chapter 5

A Model for a Complete Quality Program

In this chapter, a model is described that was developed to guide the application of the quality philosophy to research and development activities. Although I believe the model is applicable universally, it has been applied only to research and development programs so far. In order to help understand this model and to show how to use it, a few more terms must be introduced, along with a description of the "parameters of quality."

More Definitions

Six additional terms are used in this section: system, process, input, output, provider, and receiver. The first four come from the technical world and should be familiar to students of fluid mechanics, thermodynamics, or electronics. The last two are more common in the management community and should be recognized by people in purchasing and legal departments.

A *system* is an assembly of people, time, money, information, energy, and things that causes inputs to be transformed by a process into outputs. Systems can be either *open* or *closed*. Open systems permit matter and energy to cross their boundaries. Closed systems do not permit the transfer of matter or energy across their boundaries.

A *process* is anything that causes a system to change from one state to another.

An *input* is any entity (e.g., raw material, supplies, or feed stock) that enters a system to be acted upon by the process.

An *output* is any entity (e.g., goods and services, deliverables, and products) that is produced by the process and that leaves the system.

A *provider* is anyone who provides inputs to the system. *Vendors* are those providers with whom there is a contractual relationship and with whom money or other good and valuable considerations are exchanged. *Supplier* and *giver* are other terms used for provider.

A *receiver* is anyone who receives output from the system. *Customers* are those receivers with whom there is a contractual relationship and with whom money or other good and valuable considerations are exchanged. *Recipient* and *client* are other terms used for receiver.

The Parameters of Quality

The purpose of this section is to describe the basic parameters that need to be considered in developing a quality program. The application of these parameters is discussed in Chapter 7, "Applying the Quality Model." Just six basic parameters are used to identify the categories of interest: people, time, money, information, energy, and things (see Fig. 5.1). There are, of course, many other possible variations for the basic parameters of quality; however, it is convenient at this point simply to use the first five categories above and lump everything else under "things." When confronted with a specific application, the things category can be subdivided further.

People. The transaction is used as a model, and starts with the people involved. The people involved in this model are illus-

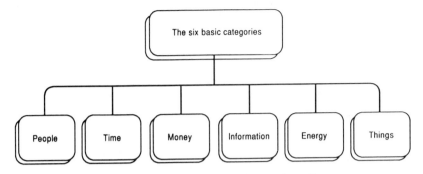

FIGURE 5.1. The six parameters or categories of quality.

trated in Fig. 5.2. The transaction, in its simplest form, involves one person giving a product to another person. The product can be either a good or a service. Consistent with the definitions in the preceding section, the person who receives the product is called the receiver and the one who provides it is the provider. Customers are a special class of receivers and vendors are a special class of providers. Customers and vendors are those entities who exchange money with the provider and as such create a special contractual relationship. To complete the model, three other groups of people must be included: helpers, stakeholders, and referees. In all of these cases, the use of the term "person" (or "people") can be expanded to mean entire organizations. For instance, in the case of a consumer product, the person generating the output can be the company producing the item.

Helpers are those people who assist the provider in creating the product. In an old-fashioned blacksmith shop, the helper was often a boy or young man who wanted to learn the trade. These apprentices did everything from cleaning the forge and tending the fire to heavy hammering under the guidance of the master blacksmith. In a modern company, the helpers include all the line and staff personnel who assist in the creation of the product. For a research or development department, the primary helpers are often such people as librarians, word processors, fabrication and maintenance personnel, and, hopefully, quality specialists.

Stakeholders include everyone who has a peripheral interest

FIGURE 5.2.   People involved in the transaction model.

in the transaction. Examples include such diverse groups as the stockholders in a corporation and the neighbors of a chemical processing plant.

Referees are those individuals or groups who create and administer rules and regulations. They include such groups as the U.S. Congress and the American Society for Testing Materials. A somewhat broader definition also would include public interest groups like the Sierra Club.

Time. Time is perhaps the most interesting category. When dealing with sponsored research, which often has externally imposed deadlines, time also can be one of the most important considerations in a technical program. Properly understood and utilized, it can provide a valuable yardstick for evaluating one aspect of research and development work both for the provider and the receiver of the work. Time can be described in two ways, linear or circular. Linear time commonly is used to measure the progress of tasks, projects, and programs. However, most companies also operate in a temporally circular world of annual budgets and recurring progress reports. Both aspects of time are significant and must be accommodated in any quality program.

Money. In most industrial settings, money is of concern mainly as budgets and costs, as opposed to the financial industry, in which cash, gold, or negotiable instruments are the primary merchandise handled. The quality issues usually involve obtaining proper funding to accomplish the tasks required and then ensuring that expenditures are in keeping with the funding. The concept of the open system is very useful in identifying the pertinent factors to be addressed and seeing how the flow of information behaves. The open system is used to model the money category (see Fig. 5.3). For personal finances, the input is generally in the form of a salary plus income from investments, outputs are the monies spent, and savings are storage terms in the equation describing the system. For a typical research project, a single input generally occurs at the start of a fiscal year as an annual budget allowance. Outputs are described monthly as periodic cost sheets. The perceived quality of research and development programs often is affected by the conformance of the expenditures to the budget.

Information. It has been said often that our culture is in an information age, a post-industrial age. So, creating and utilizing information should be simple and straightforward. But, in fact, managing information is one of the major challenges facing most companies today. This parameter describes one of the most extensive categories in the list of quality attributes. It must include not only the direct information obtained as a result of the technical investigations, but also the secondary information relating to such things as personnel records, safety documents,

FIGURE 5.3. Open system representation of a money transaction.

and cost reports. In the research environment, the common categories of information that should be considered include references to previous studies and other input information, data obtained during the course of the investigation, such records as laboratory notebooks kept during the course of the study, and reports and other documents reporting progress and results.

As with money, the open system is used to model this category (see Fig. 5.4). Information is often the most important output of research and development programs. The quality of existing information, which serves as input to the program, is of fundamental importance for planning and execution of the work. The output information has two significant aspects, its form and its substance. The substance of the information is the reason for doing the work and should be the primary basis for evaluating the program. The form of the reports containing the technical information should have significance only in that the work should be presented in such a manner that the results are easy to understand and are professional in appearance.

Energy. The next category is energy, one that almost always is omitted from lists of factors to be monitored in a quality program. Not only is it an obvious factor to include for a thermodynamicist, but for a utility it is the principal product, and in many industries energy is an ever-increasing factor in terms of both cost and availability. Once again, the open system is used to describe energy considerations. In this instance, the open system concept is used in one of its classical technical forms. In an automobile, energy flows into the system in the form of chemical energy from gasoline. The chemical energy is converted to thermal energy in the system. Finally, a portion of the thermal energy is converted to mechanical energy, which leaves the system as motion of the car. The remaining thermal energy leaves the system as waste heat. Similarly, in a coal-fired power plant, chemical energy enters the plant in the coal and is con-

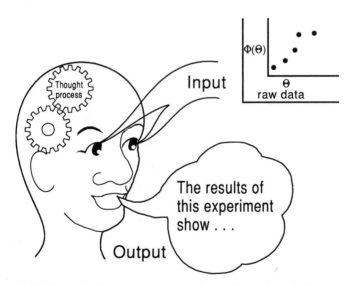

FIGURE 5.4. Open system representation of an information model for a research project.

verted to thermal energy in the firebox. The thermal energy then is converted, in part, into electrical energy, which leaves the plant on electrical transmission lines. The portion of the thermal energy that is not converted to electricity is discharged to the environment as waste heat. A simplified systems analysis for a power plant is shown in Fig. 5.5.

As environmental and conservation concerns become more significant, the energy-related aspects of research and development activities will become even more important. More work will have to be directed to improving the energy-effectiveness of products and processes, and more attention will have to be paid to the energy consumed as we carry out technical programs.

Things. The category, "things," is the most extensive on our list and, for most industrial settings, it can be subdivided logically

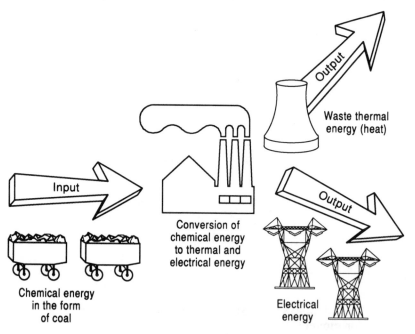

FIGURE 5.5. Open system model for energy conversion.

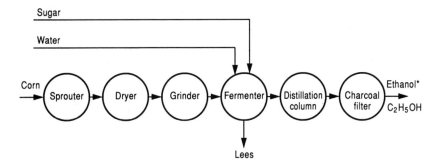

*Sometimes referred to in the South as sour mash whiskey

FIGURE 5.6. Open system representation of a chemical process in the form of a flow sheet.

into materials, equipment, and facilities. *Materials* are essentially the components that go into the product; the *equipment* is used to produce the product; and the *facilities* are the places in which the work is done. Materials sometimes are subdivided further into *direct materials* (the elements that actually make up the product and that are listed on a bill of material) and *indirect materials* or *supplies* (the elements needed to conduct the business that do not show up in the product, such as office supplies or janitorial supplies). The things category is the most variable from task to task and, in Chapter 7, the section, "The Work to be Done," shows several examples of its use in a variety of situations. Again, the open system provides the model for this parameter. An example of a model of an open system that is used widely in chemical engineering is the flow sheet. A flow sheet is used to describe the flow of process materials through the pieces of equipment in a chemical plant. A simplified chemical flow sheet is shown in Fig. 5.6.

The System Concept

A brief definition of *system* was given at the beginning of this chapter and the concept was used to explain some of the ideas in the preceding section; here, the definition is expanded. The use of the concept of the system is one of the key tenets of the approach to quality presented here.

The idea of the system has different embodiments in different fields of science and engineering. One typical definition in thermodynamics is: "The system is . . . the region where transfers of mass and energy are to be studied" (1, p. 26). Another definition for *system* is: "a part of the continuum which is separated from the rest of the continuum for convenience in the formulation of a problem" (2, p. 18).

The concept of the system used here is an extension of the concept used in thermodynamics and other scientific fields, but it does not need to be as rigorous. In technical studies in which objective, quantitative results are needed, it is necessary to be exact in defining the system boundaries and the transfers of matter and energy across them. For our purposes, this is not necessary. As we look at the interactions between connected subsystems, we even can shift the emphasis to different quantities if doing so focuses attention on the desired issues.

The basic concept is quite simple and is shown in Fig. 5.7. All things that go into the system are considered inputs. In addition to matter and energy, which are the classic entities that are studied in systems analysis, we also investigate information as it flows into and out of systems. Anything that leaves the system is considered an output. In most systems, an agent working within the system acts on the inputs and causes some change. This change is referred to as a *transformation*. In some

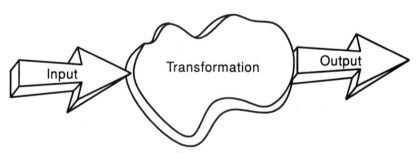

FIGURE 5.7. The basic representation of an open system.

areas, especially in the study of circuit theory in the field of electronics, an additional factor exists, a feedback loop associated with the system. We will consider this aspect a little further on.

Systems can become subsystems of larger systems and, conversely, any system can be broken down into smaller subsystems. For instance, a common transportation system, an automobile, can be broken down into the coach system, guidance system, and propulsion system. Each of these can in turn be subdivided into smaller systems. At the same time, an individual automobile is a subsystem in a community's transportation system.

A certain amount of liberty is taken in using the systems concept in this book. Mathematical calculations are not performed with the system models; a methodology is not developed that is amenable to computer analysis and application. Rather, the concept is used to illustrate the flow of people, things, time, energy, money, and information in a quality program, and to show how these parameters interact and influence one another.

The Complete Quality System

In this section, six systems are identified and described that become the subsystems of a model of a complete quality system. The six systems described perform the functions of preparation, execution, evaluation, reward, improvement, and correction. These systems have been described and studied independently in the past by various experts in the quality and management fields. However, for me, one of the "Eureka!" experiences that technical people have from time to time occurred when I saw how these systems fit together and interact. The turning point in my ability to understand and use quality principles and tools came when this interrelation occurred to me. It is hoped that the explanation here will help the readers find something of that same unification so that the ideas presented in this book can be applied to the readers' own situations.

Preparation, execution, and evaluation. To accomplish any task, three basic steps must be carried out: preparation, execution, and evaluation. This sequence of steps is represented in Fig. 5.8 by the three systems in series. Even though the first and last systems in the illustration frequently are overlooked, they do exist and need to be included in every quality program.

Every activity, no matter how simple, requires some preparation. One of the major factors leading to the success of large projects is the preparation done before the work actually is started. In this phase, the planning is performed. Good planning is critical to doing a job right the first time. The generation of a plan is a key element of the preparation step; however, preparation also includes gathering the equipment, facilities, materials and supplies, personnel, finances, and information needed in the program. Perhaps the most important detail in this phase is the identification of the requirements for the finished product and the factoring of these requirements into the plans for the execution step.

The execution system has been the focus of the engineering and manufacturing organizations in most companies. In this system, the items traditionally considered as inputs are converted to outputs by means of what commonly are called *processes*. In other words, processes are those actions that cause the trans-

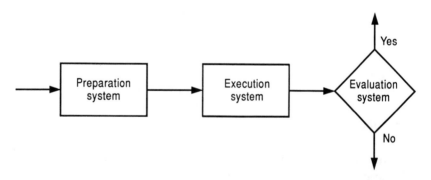

FIGURE 5.8. The three fundamental systems involved in accomplishing any task.

formation of inputs into outputs. In a research or development organization, the technical work is accomplished in the execution system.

The evaluation system historically has been identified mainly with inspection and quality control in the manufacturing industry, and has received the bulk of attention from the quality profession. During the evaluation phase, we are concerned with assessing the conformance to standards, whether we are considering a manufacturing process, the delivery of a service, the construction of a facility, or the performance of a research program.

Although evaluations traditionally have been done by the organization producing the output, it now is beginning to be recognized that all the receivers of outputs from the organization are performing their own evaluations of those outputs. Evaluations performed by the same organization that did the execution usually are referred to as in-house inspections. This type of evaluation is important in that it provides a fairly reliable method for assuring that the outputs conform to applicable codes and standards. Evaluations by external groups may be formal or informal, obvious or subtle. Customers obviously evaluate an organization's products each time a purchase is made. Many companies currently are attempting to obtain better information from their customers to help in the design and delivery of the company's products. Environmental groups, conservation groups, and citizens' groups increasingly are becoming involved in the evaluation of the waste products from companies. In addition to the internal evaluations done by employees of a company, external evaluators may be brought in by the company's management to perform certain types of special evaluations. One common form of external group used in evaluating research and development results is the advisory group. Another form of external evaluation found in the scientific and technical fields is the peer review.

Regardless of how an evaluation is performed or who performs it, the evaluation ultimately should focus on answering such questions as: Does this output conform to requirements? Is this product fit for its intended use? Does it conform to the appropriate criteria or standards? The answers to these kinds of questions will be either yes or no.

Reward and improvement systems. The answers derived from the evaluation system will lead to other systems that are considered now. If the answers are yes, the product will be delivered to the next receiver in the chain (see Fig. 5.9). In addition to the delivery of the product, in an ideal system the people involved in the successful completion of the task are rewarded, and everyone involved looks for ways to do things better the next time. The reward system can take a wide variety of forms and should be consistent with the type of work being done and the impact of the work on the whole enterprise. I believe an important aspect of a reward system is the message sent to employees that their contributions are important to the success of the business. Rewards and other forms of recognition can be simple or elaborate, but they should not be neglected. If we expect people to put forth extra effort to search for ways to improve products

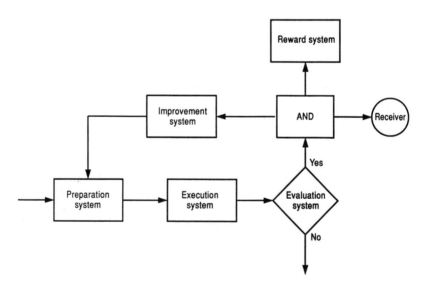

FIGURE 5.9. Addition of the reward and improvement systems to the quality model.

and processes, we must be willing to put forth extra effort to acknowledge their contributions.

Too often, if a system is operating without significant problems, we hear the comment, "If it ain't broke, don't fix it," and nothing is done to look for ways to make improvements. The appropriate response should be, "If it isn't perfect (and nothing ever is), how can we make it better?" This response should apply to every situation, regardless of the nature of the work. For example, in any technical program, more experiments always need to be performed, more information needs to be gleaned.

It is important to emphasize that a constant improvement program in no way implies any criticism of previous work. On the contrary, improvements should be viewed as increments in performance and quality above an already okay situation.

In a manufacturing plant, quality circles could be put to use in the improvement system. As is explained in Chapter 6, similar approaches can be utilized in technical work also.

One important point to note is the use of the receiver's requirements as inputs both to the evaluation system and the preparation system. The customer's or other receiver's requirements are just beginning to receive the attention they deserve. A significant amount of study currently is being directed toward finding ways to determine just what it is that a customer wants. The research in this field is finding that the receiver has both objective and subjective criteria for evaluating a product, and quite often neither type is well described in the receiver's mind. This model points out the importance of including all the receiver's requirements in planning as well as in the final evaluation. Some of the techniques for ascertaining these criteria are described in the next chapter.

Correction system. Unfortunately, there are times when the product does not conform to specifications and a correction system must be utilized. When this happens, the last system in our model comes into play (Fig. 5.10). In the correction part of a quality program, some of the more important lessons learned can be identified and factored into the system so that past errors

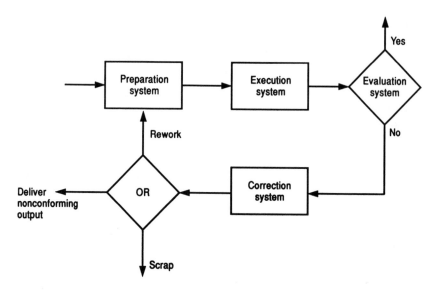

FIGURE 5.10. The correction system is the final part of the quality model.

are not repeated. The diamond at the left of the figure shows the usual options available to a producer when products are created that do not conform to specifications. The output can be scrapped, reworked, or delivered to the receiver as nonconforming product. If nonconforming output is a major part of a company's output, the costs of nonconformance can be appreciable. Scrap and rework are areas in which the costs of poor quality are most significant and in which there is the greatest potential for cost savings.

Feedback. At this point, you will recognize that there are two feedback loops, one shown in Fig. 5.9 and one shown in Fig. 5.10. Although these loops are not the classical feedback loops found in control theory, the lines with arrows on the ends do point out how information from one part of a program can influence other parts. An important aspect of the value of feedback is in the lessons learned. Many large companies (especially companies doing business with the federal government) are becoming sensitive to the meaning of the phrase "lessons learned"; as technology becomes more complex and the cost of errors grows, it is becoming increasingly important to learn from mistakes and to avoid making the same ones again.

The complete quality model. The sections above provide the basic description of the complete quality model (CQM) (Fig. 5.11). This model should provide a conceptual picture of how the various elements of a quality program are tied together and the key interactions. This model is used throughout the rest of this book to illustrate how the various activities in research and development programs are interconnected with the elements of a quality program.

Relationship to Previous Work

In the recent past, the focus of the quality profession has seemed to move from the evaluation step (inspection and quality control) to the execution step (control of processes), and, most recently, to the preparation step (in which the emphasis is on sound planning). The CQM takes all these points of view into account. It recognizes the importance of the standards not only of customers, but of all the individuals and groups who are receivers of any of the outputs of the system. Furthermore, it acknowledges the importance of continuous improvement and shows clearly how and where such activities fit into a complete quality program. The model shows where corrections belong in a total quality program and where the costs related to quality in terms of scrap, rework, or delivery of nonconforming products fit into the overall picture. In summary, the model includes the majority of the concepts in the current quality literature and fits them into one simple framework. The benefit of such a framework is that it allows a clear and simple view of the interactions among the various subsystems.

One valuable perspective about quality problems is given by Juran, Gryna, and Bingham in their description of chronic and sporadic problems (3). In the context of the model, chronic

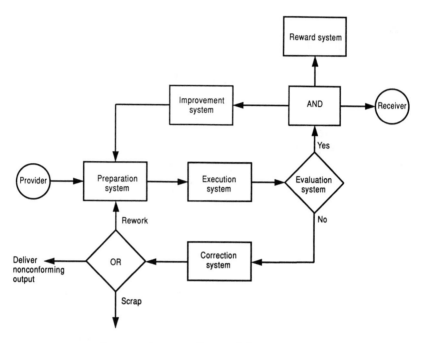

FIGURE 5.11. The complete quality model.

problems are those that can be dealt with in the improvement loop. In this case, the execution system seems to be under control and there is little motivation to fix something that is not broken. However, it is here that small, constant improvements can be made. The sporadic problems are represented in the lower loop. Dealing with the chronic problems is often very challenging, especially in mature technologies. However, the chronic problems of a company are often sources of very fruitful work for the technical staffs. Working on sporadic problems is usually simpler since the problems are better defined and this type of task often can be challenging and enjoyable. Members of the technical staff frequently are called upon to assist in this type of problem. Unfortunately, in most organizations, it seems that people often are rewarded better for solving the sporadic problems than for producing good products and making small but steady improvements to the chronic problems.

Deming's plan–do–check–act philosophy also is present in the CQM (4). The model is a more comprehensive approach to these activities. Planning is one part of preparation, doing is synonymous with execution, evaluation includes checking, and both the improvement and correction loops are ways of acting.

Chapter 7 uses the background presented in the previous chapters, along with the tools discussed in Chapter 6, to show how a quality program actually can be put together for research and development organizations.

References

1. Edward F. Obert, *Thermodynamics* (New York: McGraw-Hill, 1948).

2. Vedat S. Arpaci, *Conduction Heat Transfer* (Reading, MA: Addison-Wesley, 1966).

3. J. M. Juran, Frank M. Gryna, Jr., and R. S. Bingham, Jr., eds., *Juran's Quality Control Handbook*, 3d ed. (New York: McGraw-Hill, 1974), pp. 2–14, 2–15.

4. Ted A. Lowe and Joseph M. Mazzeo, "Crosby, Deming, Juran: Three Preachers, One Religion," *Quality* 25:22–25 (September 1986).

Chapter **6**

A Review of Quality Tools

Those who practice the quality craft, like other "craftspeople," have a collection of tools that they use. This collection is quite extensive; in this chapter, the diversity of tools employed in the quality craft is discussed and their uses outlined. There is not enough space to describe them in detail, but references are provided for those readers who wish additional information.

First, a word of caution is necessary. Anyone who has taken the most elementary manual arts course is aware that the use of improper tools is not only awkward and inefficient, but also sometimes dangerous. In the quality field, the same opportunities for misuse exist; control charts are not needed for every operation and a Pareto analysis cannot solve every defect problem. A general overview of the available tools should help an individual faced with a quality problem select the appropriate tool. Also, showing some of the similarities in the ways in which tools are used in research and development and in more traditional work environments should enhance the dialogue between research and development practitioners and quality professionals.

The list of tools discussed in a book of this size obviously cannot be complete. Most of the common ones plus a few personal favorites are covered. Technically trained individuals should be acquainted already with most of the basics discussed in this chapter. Cartesian plots to present data, the fundamental concepts of statistics, and the techniques for problem solving are used in virtually all scientific and engineering fields.

The results of recent studies on how the brain processes data imply that one part of the brain processes visual data, and that this processing is accomplished fairly easily. Another part processes numerical information, which is a more difficult operation. Both numerical and visual tools are valuable to research and development workers. Effective quality programs will utilize the strengths of all the appropriate tools available. Mathematical equations will give one perspective on a set of data, a plot of the points will give another. Good technical information must be built on precise, accurate data that is properly analyzed and presented, and taken with appropriately calibrated measuring instruments in well-designed experiments. The visualization tools are helpful in planning experimental programs, describing relationships between events, resolving poorly defined problems, and evaluating the performance of technical groups.

The tools employed in the quality craft can be divided into five basic categories: measurement tools, statistical tools, tools used for visualization and analysis, tools used for idea generation, and tools used for decision making. The measurement tools have been in existence almost since humans became tool users; weights and measures have been with us since antiquity. The statistical tools and tools used for visualization and analysis are more recent developments, evolving over the last 200 years in conjunction with the growth of Western mathematics. Finally, the tools used for idea generation and decision making have been recognized only in the last century and have paralleled the growth of management as a separate discipline. Most of the tools described in this chapter can be used for both administrative and operational purposes. Many tools are familiar from their technical applications; however, their use in developing an understanding of the quality of research and development activities is new and incompletely understood.

Measurement Tools

The tools in the measurement category are used to measure the characteristics of a product, regardless of whether the product is an item being manufactured, a service being delivered, or research data being obtained. In manufacturing, construction, and fabrication organizations in which the products are tangible goods, the tools in this category commonly are associated with the field of metrology. Metrological tools provide the initial measurements of the properties of the item being evaluated. Common examples of these tools are micrometers, pH meters, voltmeters, Geiger counters, and thermometers. The results are predominantly numerical and quantitative and, in many manufacturing applications, routine measurements are being done automatically. An infrastructure exists for the field of metrology, complete with equipment manufacturers, learned journals, and professional societies.

In nonmanufacturing industries in which the product is a service (a less tangible commodity), micrometers are not available to gauge customer approval, and the concept of metrology seems out of place. Nonetheless, deliverers of services must make measurements of aesthetic, temporal, and economic dimensions. In this situation, the tools include questionnaires, surveys, interviews, stopwatches, and budget sheets, and the information obtained makes up the raw data from which the quality of the service can be determined. Many tools for use in the management field are being adapted to these applications, and a new era in the field of surveying is emerging (1,2).

The classical concept of metrology appears somewhat foreign to research and development, too. However, similarities do exist between manufacturing and research and development in respect to the types of measurements that are made, who makes them, how the measurements are used, who evaluates the measurements, and the physical parameters that are measured. The basic issues in both environments include use of appropriate equipment, training for the people using the equipment, and calibration. Thus, the measurements made in an experimental system in a research or development laboratory in many ways are similar to the dimensional measurements of a manufactured part made in a factory. One difference between the measurement equipment found in a laboratory and that found in a factory is that laboratory instrumentation must be more versatile and consequently more complex because in research the values expected from the measurements usually are not known ahead of time. The laboratory worker must determine the precision and accuracy requirements for the measuring instruments to be used in an experiment. In addition, the researcher must decide what kind of calibration program is needed for the system. In contrast, in a mass-production situation, the measurements are well defined ahead of time, and instrument calibrations commonly are handled by special support organizations.

Statistical Tools

The dictionary defines *statistics* as "a branch of mathematics dealing with the collection, analysis, interpretation, and presentation of masses of numerical data" (3). The statistical tools include the mathematics needed to manipulate the data and the associated graphical tools to display the information and assist in seeing the relationships inherent in the numbers. The statistical tools of interest in this book can be divided into three broad groups: tools used to design experiments, tools used to monitor the acquisition of data, and tools used to analyze experimental data.

The first group comprises the tools used to plan experimental programs. These tools are of interest to many potential users. In traditional manufacturing applications, they are used most often to find ways to improve existing processes. The same tools are useful in optimizing any experimental program, especially when applied before data collection begins. They are valuable at the start of an experimental program as an aid to define the number of experimental runs that will be needed in order to obtain a desired degree of accuracy. They also are helpful in development programs involved in the analysis and improvement of existing production processes, particularly in the chemical-process industry. Some of the statistical methods are quite simple, others extremely complex. The approach taken by Taguchi emphasizes simplicity at the expense of rigor (4). It appears to have its greatest utility in development programs seeking improvements in existing processes. The more rigorous Design of Experiments techniques provide more quantitative information but require more mathematical knowledge (5,6).

The second group of tools comprises those found in traditional quality control activities. Here, measurement data are obtained from the metrologists, analyzed, and presented in the form of run charts or control charts. The mathematics involved is fairly simple, and the techniques can be taught to most employees and utilized in production operations. This type of statistical analysis is most helpful in repetitive operations, and the techniques are useful primarily for processes that are in statistical control. In research and development programs, their main utility is in keeping track of experimental data as it is being acquired. Many standard texts cover the application of statistics to quality issues and new ones are appearing constantly. This field was defined by Shewhart, whose work still forms the basis of statistical quality control (7). Among the more recent publications, the texts by Burr (8), Grant and Leavenworth (9), and Montgomery (10) provide a good cross section of information from statisticians, economists, and engineers.

The third group of tools contains those used to analyze data and includes such techniques as least-squares fitting and multivariate analysis. This is perhaps the area of statistical analysis most familiar to technical people involved in experimental studies. Indeed, many of the techniques have evolved from needs expressed by experimentalists. In their simplest form, the methods provide the algorithm for drawing the familiar least-squares line through a set of data points. The more sophisticated techniques allow a researcher to find relations among large numbers of variables. For these methods to be of optimum use, the data should have been obtained from a designed experiment. Although an experienced statistician can determine the relationships among variables from almost any set of data, the amount of information can be enhanced greatly and the amount of work greatly reduced if the experiment is designed properly ahead of time. It generally is helpful to obtain the services of a good statistician at the very beginning of any program that will involve the accumulation of a significant amount of data. Reference 11 is a general text that deals with the analysis of data and is attuned to the needs of the experimentalist.

Computers are being used in many ways to assist with the statistical analysis of data. If a computer is being used to help with data acquisition, it is possible to include programs that will do statistical analysis as the data is acquired. When this is done, the experimentalist is functioning in a manner similar to any production situation in which run charts, control charts, and other statistical charts are produced as the work progresses. In this way, it is possible to be sure that the experimental system is performing as desired, and that the results will be useful. Computers also are used for data analysis, using any of the standard programming languages (such as BASIC or FORTRAN). Subroutines for these languages exist that describe virtually all of the statistical calculations of interest to scientists and engineers. Finally, many software packages are available to assist with statistical analyses. These packages range from personal computer spreadsheets, databases, and graphics packages, which contain statistical functions as one part of the set of algorithms available to the user, to comprehensive personal computer and mainframe programs (such as SAS®, from the SAS Institute, Inc., Cary, North Carolina) that are capable of extensive statistical analysis (12).

Tools for Visualizing and Analyzing Information

The purpose of the tools discussed in this section is to help research and development workers understand information. These tools will make it easier for the right side of the brain to participate in the analysis of data. They are based on the premise that one picture is worth several equations, many data points, or a thousand words. Most of the tools are familiar in one form or another to technical people and are grouped into four categories: data display tools, tree structures, flowcharts, and matrix tools.

Displaying data. The usefulness of plotting data to display relationships between variables and as an aid in understanding the data is well understood and is used widely in the research and development world. The methods used are mostly variations of the familiar Cartesian plot, or x-y graph. Some of the variations are designed for special uses in quality programs.

One of the principal uses of Cartesian plots is to display the data from experiments and calculations. Scientists and engineers make use of a rich variety of plots of this nature using not only linear scales, but also logarithmic, polar, and other coordinate systems. There are numerous texts that cover the technical and esthetic aspects of the graphical presentation of data (13–15). Many computer programs also are available to assist with the routine creation of various types of graphs. Some are incorporated into word-processing software (16) and others are part of general graphics programs (17). The technically trained worker often can assist the quality organization with ideas for presenting data.

One use of Cartesian plots is to display the results of statistical studies of information. In a quality context, when the technique is used to plot data as a function of time or of a part number, the resulting graph is called a *run chart* (Fig. 6.1). If the system being studied is in statistical control, control limits can be added and the chart then is referred to as a *control chart* (Fig. 6.2). These types of charts have been used extensively in manufacturing and continuous-process situations to assure that the process parameters of interest are staying within control limits. Control charts add a degree of rigor to the run chart by showing when action should be taken. Another statistical tool is the *scatter diagram*, in which data points of two variables are plotted to reveal any correlation between them.

Run charts and control charts are of use to technical workers in a variety of research and development activities. Run charts are common in many development activities in the

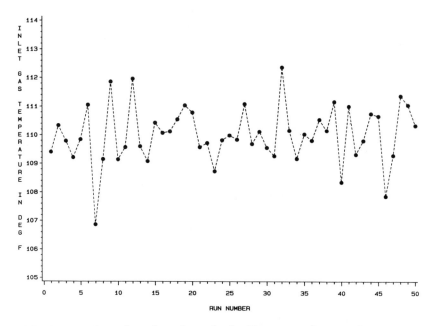

FIGURE 6.1. Run chart for a hypothetical heat transfer experiment.

chemical-process industry. For instance, they can be used in chemical pilot plants to assure that the processes and outputs are in control, and in experimental research projects to keep track of calibrations on instruments. Control charts commonly are found in repetitive, large-volume environments because they are most useful in situations in which the process is well characterized and many units are produced. Control charts are of interest to the research and development community in relation to any analytical work being supplied to them. For example, research and development workers must be able to understand and interpret the control chart information generated by the analytical chemistry department so that the researchers can evaluate the quality of the information based on the analysis.

The common least-squares plot in which the variation of the data around a predetermined type of curve is minimized can be regarded as a generalization of the control chart. The technique used to calculate least-squares lines is referred to as *regression analysis*. This and many similar techniques for analyzing and plotting data are contained in Ref. 18.

In addition to the use of Cartesian plots for rigorous data analysis, they also can be helpful in solving some of the more subjective problems that arise in the course of research and development projects. Quite often when unexpected phenomena occur, insight can be gained simply by plotting the various parameters involved and observing the trends instead of each point independently.

In many research and development projects, *x-y* plots are the principal tools for analyzing the data and transmitting the data to the next user. Technical experts tend to think graphically even if their final product is an equation. Data acquisition is becoming more automated, allowing computers to receive the data, analyze it, and write the equation; however, the mature research or development worker will want to see a plot of the raw data in order to visualize as much as possible about the

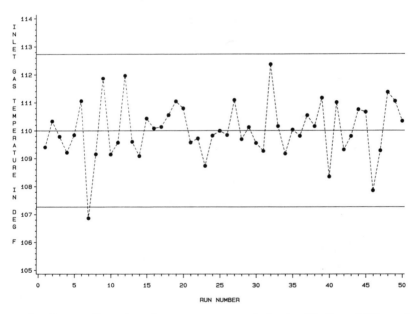

FIGURE 6.2. Run chart becomes a control chart with the addition of control limits.

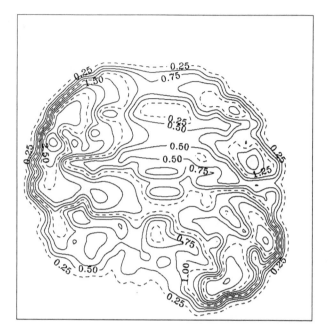

FIGURE 6.3. Contour plot of optical characteristics of laser system element.

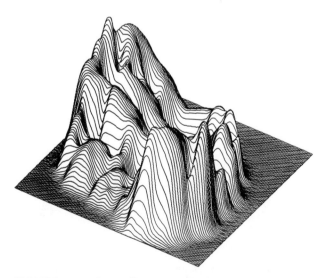

FIGURE 6.4. Three-dimensional plot of optical characteristics of laser system element.

work, and thus achieve a better feel for it. Useful insights often are gained by noticing a small curvature in a set of data that was assumed to be linear, or seeing what appears to be a change in slope at some unexpected point.

So far, we have considered just the relationships between two variables. In many situations, it is desirable to show the relationship among three or more variables. Although we must work in two dimensions on paper, several techniques exist for representing more than two variables on paper. The simplest technique is to draw a contour plot (see Fig. 6.3). Alternatively, it is possible to represent the three coordinates on the paper in the manner shown in Fig. 6.4 and many computer software programs are available now to do just that (17).

Bar graphs are most useful for displaying data that can be subdivided into discrete units. The independent variable can represent either consecutive intervals of a single variable or a variety of attributes. Bar graphs showing the relative significance of a number of factors are frequently used in development activities to categorize failures to see what patterns, if any, are present.

One type of bar graph commonly used in quality studies is the *histogram*, which shows the numbers of events falling into

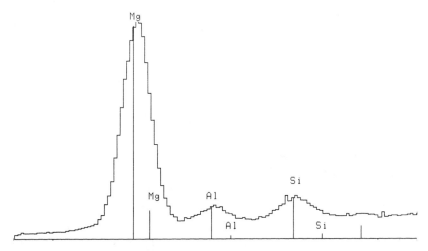

FIGURE 6.5. Histogram of spectroscopic data, showing frequencies of counts in subdivisions of the energy range.

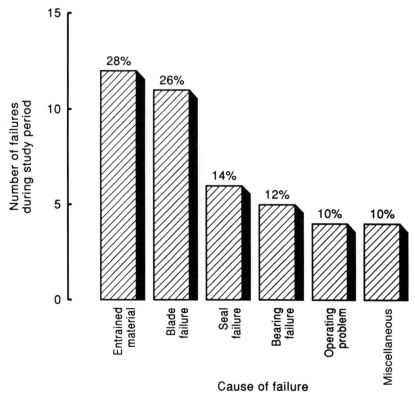

FIGURE 6.6. Pareto plot of compressor system failures.

different intervals. An example of a histogram taken from the field of spectroscopy is shown in Fig. 6.5.

When the bars in a graph are arranged in descending order, the result is often referred to as a *Pareto diagram*. This type of presentation helps identify the few causes that are influencing a system the most. Figure 6.6 shows a Pareto diagram prepared as part of a development program that looked at ways to improve the performance of seals in a chemical plant by reducing the failure rate. Ishikawa presents a comprehensive introduction to histograms and Pareto diagrams (19), and routines also are available in most spreadsheet, graphical, and some word-processing software for producing these types of plots.

Pie charts are most useful when it is necessary to convey the idea of the fraction of a total amount divided among a set of subdivisions. They often are used as a supplement to a bar graph or Pareto diagram when a sense of the proportion of various factors aids understanding. One typical technical application is given in Fig. 6.7, which presents the fraction of seal failures in Fig. 6.6 in pie-chart form.

Tree structures. "Next week we've got to get organized." Does this sound familiar? The need to get organized is basic for accomplishing any task, particularly when talking about quality. The reason is that quality is based on a comparison to standards, and an organized approach to defining the standards and making comparisons to them is essential. An organized approach to comparing facts and results to standards is needed in each of the systems in a quality program. The basic task of organizing is to

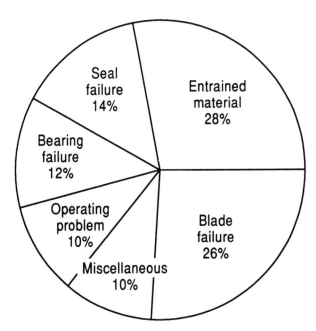

FIGURE 6.7. Pie chart representation of compressor system failures.

subdivide the area of concern into a logical set of subunits, such as the six basic categories of people, things, time, money, information, and energy.

Taxonomy and classification always have been essential parts of scientific investigation and can be represented in three basic formats: the outline, the breakdown structure, and the Ishikawa (or fishbone) diagram. Figure 6.8 shows examples of the three forms. Topologically, all three are identical, and computer programs are available to create outlines (16) and breakdown structures (20). It should be just a matter of time until the fishbone diagram is available in computer form, if not already available.

Each of these formats has its own place in a quality program; each is suited for particular applications. The table of contents for a book is more useful in outline form than in fishbone form. The interrelationships among workers show up better in a type of breakdown structure called an organization chart than in an outline. Fishbone diagrams are used most often to chart the possible causes of problems and then are called cause-and-effect diagrams. The simplest organizational tool is the list, which is merely a one-dimensional outline. Ishikawa points out the utility of having a well-thought-out list of things to do before starting any experimental program. ''Do'' lists and checklists are always useful as memory aids.

Flowcharts. Flowcharts similar to those used by chemical engineers and their myriad variations that have evolved over the years are among the most useful quality tools for scientific workers. They provide a simple visual tool for exploring complex relationships among entities. In their traditional form, flowcharts are used widely in the chemical-process industry and in computer programming. In these applications, the technique is highly developed, and international standards exist for determining which symbols to use to represent various concepts. The use of flowcharts is growing in many other technical areas and their utility has been recognized in the management area. The concept is deceptively simple. One simply draws a series of circles or boxes or any other closed figure and con-

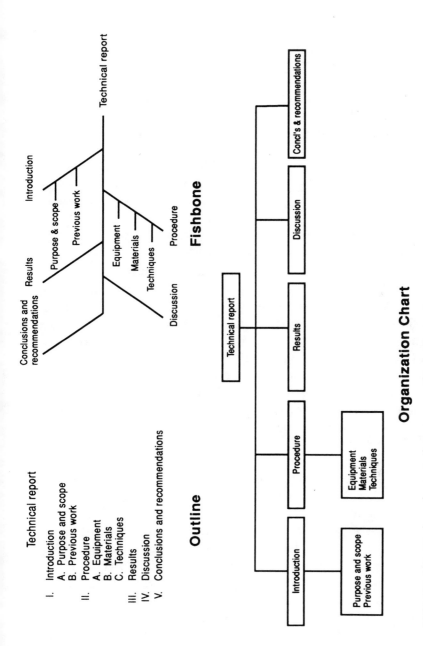

Fishbone

Outline

Technical report

I. Introduction
   A. Purpose and scope
   B. Previous work
II. Procedure
   A. Equipment
   B. Materials
   C. Techniques
III. Results
IV. Discussion
V. Conclusions and recommendations

Organization Chart

FIGURE 6.8. Various formats for representing a taxonomy.

91

nects them with various kinds of lines. A typical example is shown in Fig. 5.5. The idea is to show how the items or activities in the boxes interact with one another. If the lines have arrowheads on one end, they imply that what happens in one box affects the next. The use of flowcharts is becoming so ubiquitous that they are used almost without thought. The flowchart is a classic example of a tool that can be helpful at both the technical level (as in describing a chemical process) and at the administrative level (as when laying out the sequence of steps that must be taken to get ready to perform an experiment). The use of flowcharts in these applications is done almost intuitively and often mentally. The advantage of committing the flowchart to paper (or a video display terminal) is that it allows us to see the relationships among the entities of interest and often will help uncover bottlenecks and shortcuts.

Special types of flowcharts that are used to map the flow of events with time include the Program Evaluation and Review Technique (PERT) and the Critical Path Method (CPM). These similar techniques were developed in the 1950s to assist in the tracking and optimizing of major military research and development activities and commercial construction projects (21). The tasks and milestones involved in a project are identified, the time required to perform each task is estimated, and algorithms are available to show how the events must fit together for successful completion of the work. Figure 6.9 is a very simple example showing how the steps of the scientific method might be laid out in a PERT program. These techniques have been refined over the years and software now is available to perform the calculations required and produce the graphical output; the OPEN PLAN® software (WST Corporation, Houston, Texas) is a typical example (22). Five of the seven tools described in Ref. 23 can be grouped under the general category of flowcharts; they are the relations diagram, the KJ method, the systematic diagram, the process decision program chart, and the arrow diagram. The possible applications are extensive and the details are only as limited as the imagination of the individual using the techniques.

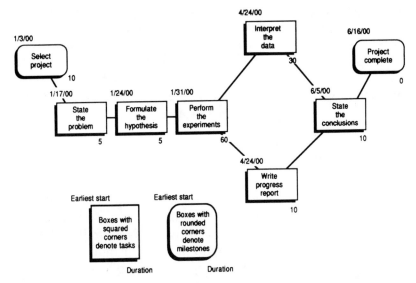

FIGURE 6.9. A PERT diagram of the scientific method.

Matrix tools. When a problem involves many variables and multiple interactions exist between the variables, it often is helpful to display the information involving the variables in the form of a matrix. A matrix is just a two-dimensional table in which the columns and rows are defined carefully. Ordinary numerical reference tables, such as tables of trigonometric functions, are simple examples. Matrices are an integral part of two of the seven new quality tools described in Ref. 23. Hauser and Clausing use the concept to build their "House of Quality," which they assert provides a "means for interfunctional planning and communication" (24, p. 63). Quality function deployment (QFD) employs matrices to compare product attributes with customer expectations (25, 26). The use of matrices as information display tools allows large amounts of information to be presented in one place in a relatively simple format.

Matrices can be used in both conceptual and mathematical applications. Their primary application in the quality field has been to handle conceptual, qualitative, and semiquantitative issues. Figure 6.10 shows an application of a matrix to the ranking of the characteristics of a new software package by a set of users. An example of a matrix familiar to technical workers is the output from a spreadsheet calculation. Utilized in this manner, a matrix can be helpful in answering the what-if questions that occur when decisions are being made about the proper course of action to be taken in a program.

Idea-Generating Tools

One of the most important tools for a research or development person is one that generates new ideas. New ideas and new avenues to explore are the stock-in-trade of research and development professionals. Those who make their living in research and development are paid to keep coming up with new ideas, hypotheses, and theories. In connection with research and de-

	Points for attribute 1				Points for attribute m	Total points
Points available	0-5				0-p	
Software package a						
. . .						
.						
Software package n						

FIGURE 6.10. Sample of a matrix for use in evaluating a set of software packages.

velopment activities, there are two aspects of the need to generate new ideas, technical and administrative. The tools described in this section therefore are not only valuable for a quality program but apply to the very nature of research and development work. In connection with the quality aspects of a program, idea-generating tools find application mainly in the preparation, improvement, and correction systems. Idea-generating tools currently are receiving attention in connection with group processes and creativity. Five tools that I have found most useful in technical work are described: group techniques, analogies, clustering, describing, and subconscious thought processes.

Group techniques. There are three common tools for developing ideas in a group: brainstorming, the nominal group technique, and the Delphi method. These methods are described in Refs. 27–29. Group techniques are useful in situations in which it is beneficial to involve several people in the resolution of a problem. My experience indicates that groups with between 6 and 20 members are most productive, with 10 to 12 members being the optimum. These tools tend to work best on nontechnical problems. They are very effective when a consensus is needed and the people involved in the generation of the ideas will be the ones who must work on the solution to the actual problem. Of the three methods, brainstorming, in which the participants meet and express their ideas freely, is the least structured and probably the least valuable. The nominal group technique and the Delphi method are designed to encourage more participation by all the members of the group and to help achieve a consensus approach to problem resolution. In both of these methods, the participants write down their ideas; in the Delphi method, they do not meet, but send in their ideas, which are collated and returned.

When technical issues are concerned, group methods can be ineffective unless the group leader is very competent at keeping a group focused. Group methods tend to be most helpful to research and development organizations in such activities as defining new areas of work for a group to pursue, scoping ideas for approaches to resolving a problem, and identifying instruments that might be used in a project. Brainstorming is not likely to resolve a major technical issue. The tools discussed in the section, "Describing Techniques," are more appropriate for this kind of task.

Analogies. A technique that I have found particularly useful when looking for new ideas or new approaches to problems is to identify one or more analogs to the original situation. An analog is simply one thing that is similar to another in one or more aspects. Analogs may be physical or conceptual. In many diverse technical fields, the physical phenomena of interest all are described by the same set of mathematical equations. For instance, the so-called potential equation $\nabla^2 \phi = 0$ describes, among other things, the flow of electricity in a conductor, the flow of thermal energy in a homogenous solid, and the flow of a special class of fluids.

When one encounters a technical problem in which the mathematics are too complex to solve directly and the nature of the problem is such that conducting experimental work on the system of interest is perhaps too expensive or dangerous, it often is possible to study an analogous system. My master's thesis was based on an analogy between soap bubbles and temperature distribution. As a result of my experience with this method of analyzing problems, I always have had a liking for the approach.

Analog computers, which were serious rivals to digital computers in the 1950s, are based on the analogies between voltages and currents in certain types of electrical circuit elements and the solutions to a wide variety of differential equations that describe many diverse physical systems. The analog timepiece (clock) uses the positions of two rotating sticks as an analog of time. As digital computers have become faster and more sophisticated, algorithms have become available for the numerical solution of mathematical problems, and the application of analog techniques has diminished. In some ways, this is unfortunate because many analog techniques gave a visual approach to the solution. This visual aspect largely is lost in the tables of numbers most computers produce. This is why many computer software programs are being written to create graphical outputs.

When attempting to find ideas for developing quality programs for research and development tasks, it is very helpful to examine the tools that have been developed for manufacturing systems and see what analogies exist in the research and development environment. Often, examining analogies also will point out areas in which real differences exist between systems. As pointed out at the beginning of this chapter, not all tools can or should be used on all problems, and an analogy can help show what are the limitations. The realization that there were similarities (an analogy) between technical seminars and quality circles led me to institute a series of technical evaluation and review meetings (TERMs) in my department. The nature of these meetings is discussed in the section on peer review in Chapter 7. A side benefit of the use of analogies such as this is that a good analogy often makes the explanation of a new idea easier. When it is possible to show likenesses between a new concept and an approach that already is understood, the acceptance of the new way is made simpler. Conversely, the lack of any analogy between the multiple outputs of the assembly line and the singular output of a research project explains why there is little to be gained by trying to apply statistical methods to research and development outputs.

I have found analogies to be useful in all six systems of the CQM. They are especially useful in finding ways of making improvements related to some of the administrative issues in research and development. For instance, when new environmental laws required more deliberate handling of waste materials in a chemistry laboratory, the initial approach was to require each chemist to be responsible for his or her own chemical waste materials. This approach seemed to be unnecessarily time consuming and was not being handled consistently. The people responsible for the organization saw some similarities between waste-handling activities and financial management and established a waste manager position similar to the organization's financial manager position. This approach has streamlined the work and made the results much more uniform.

Clustering. Clustering is a right-brain technique for developing ideas that uses a free-form visual approach to help the mind get a variety of related thoughts together so they can be put on paper with a minimum of constraint. The technique is described thoroughly in a book on creative writing by G. L. Rico (30). Dr. Rico developed the technique during her doctoral research on the writing process. She refers to clustering as a "nonlinear brainstorming process" (30, p. 28). This is another example of a tool developed for one application that has broad application in the quality field. The process allows an individual to brainstorm without the existence of a group. This approach can be very helpful when others are not available or someone needs or wants to pursue a train of thought individually. The essence of the approach is to write a word or phrase on a sheet of paper, draw a circle or oval around it, and then write whatever words or phrases come to mind in clusters around the original thought. The technique has similarities to some of the relationship diagrams in Ref. 23 and is a type of free-form outlining. It is surprising how natural and effective this approach is in coming up with new ideas. During the preparation phase of an applied-research program, the project manager developed the cluster shown in Fig. 6.11 to identify the receivers of the outputs from the program. It was interesting to see how the cluster came about almost spontaneously. One major advantage of clustering is that it releases the user from any predetermined, left-brain patterns, and lets the mind roam widely with few constraints. I am convinced that if the project manager had started with an organization chart the broad perspective made possible by the clustering would not have developed.

An additional benefit, evident to readers of Dr. Rico's book, is that once the clustering is done the mind usually is ready to commit the thought generated by the cluster into the written word with only modest effort. I have used the technique to create technical papers and as an aid in writing this book. It was particularly useful in areas in which I had not previously had to organize my thoughts on paper or in the form of visual aids.

The technique also can be used with groups. For example, it was used in one program to help identify all the requirements for evaluation that would apply to the products of the program and, again, the process proved successful. The traditional group approaches generally require a trained, experienced group to

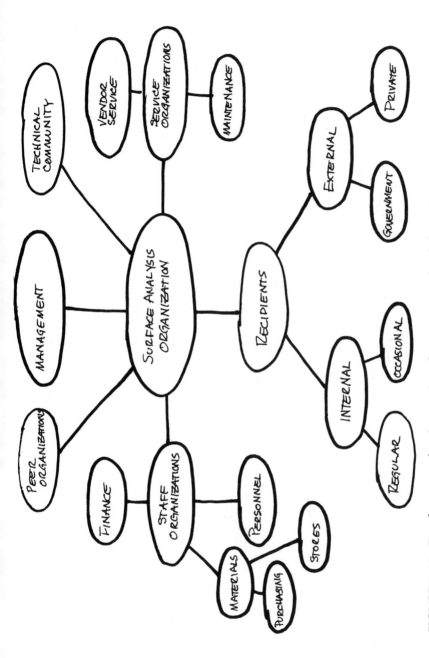

FIGURE 6.11. Development of an interaction chart, an example of clustering.

99

produce results when dealing with technical problems; clustering usually will allow a less-sophisticated group to proceed faster because the relationships among aspects of the problem become apparent as the analysis progresses.

Describing technique. Most people have had the experience of having the answer to a problem occur to them as they are in the process of describing the problem to someone else. Having noticed this happening to me several times, I have made a conscious practice of finding a sympathetic listener to talk to when confronted with a sticky problem. This approach can be formalized to include every means ranging from casual discussions to planned discussions between two people (the listener does not need to be a technical expert, although it helps if he or she can ask good questions) to presentations before groups. For technical problems, I prefer this approach to the normal group process approaches (brainstorming, nominal group technique, or Delphi method).

For the describing technique, or any group technique, to be useful in handling technical problems, a spirit of trust and cooperation must exist in the organization. First, the member of the group who is seeking help must feel secure enough to admit he or she does not have all the answers, and the other members must be mature enough not to use this type of interaction to play one-upmanship with their co-workers.

The technique also can be used to hone the solution to complex problems. In this situation, the presenter will explain the current state of understanding and the audience will test the premises and conclusions. One group, which was working on a new method for isotope separation, used the method extensively to be sure there were no gaps in their reasoning. This technique has the greatest application in improvement and correction systems.

Subconscious thought processes. Two topics are mentioned in this section, programmed dreaming and meditation. Current research into the creative process implies that many people can use these techniques for generating new ideas and finding answers to problems (31,32). The familiar approach of "sleeping on it'' can be used to advantage by certain individuals. The act of sleeping on it can be in the form of actual sleeping or in the form of meditation. Several important scientific discoveries have come to their discoverers in dreams, the most famous examples being Bohr's model of the atom and Mendeleyev's periodic table of the elements. Although dreaming and meditating are less predictable in their success than some of the other techniques mentioned, they do work for some individuals. The basic method involves formulating a problem in the mind, either before going to sleep or before a period of meditation, and then allowing the subconscious mind to work on the issue so that when the person returns to full consciousness, the conscious mind will have new insights into the issue. I have found that I often will make progress on issues that are puzzling to me during a half-hour period in the morning, just before the alarm goes off, when I am still half asleep.

Decision-Making Tools

One of the consequences of generating new ideas is the ultimate necessity of having to make decisions about which ideas to pursue and which ones to set aside. If a research project has been snagged and one of the idea-generating techniques has developed several possible approaches to follow, a decision must be made as to which one to start on first. In addition, one of the support tasks technical people often are called upon to perform is to help manufacturing organizations resolve problems that involve decisions about alternate approaches to product or process improvement. In these and similar situations, the best course of action cannot always be defined clearly and some procedure must be utilized to assist in the decision making.

People seem to have two modes of decision making, a rational approach and an intuitive approach. Some prefer and use one mode more than the other. Most rational approaches are logical extensions of the scientific method. One system for making rational decisions that seems well thought out and thoroughly described is that given by Kepner and Tregoe (33). In this system, the requirements relating to a decision are listed and divided into two categories: musts and wants. The musts are used for screening, then the remaining options are scored and ranked on the basis of wants. The system is comprehensive and provides the basis for defensible decisions when they are needed. This approach is well suited for use in groups, and can be very helpful in allowing groups to reach a consensus. It has wide potential for application in the correction system when several options to a problem are available.

Several recent articles have reported that many top managers use their intuition as a major tool in decision making. The hunch is becoming legitimized in the boardroom. However, there are those who would like to understand the process better in order to devise procedures for the gut-level feelings. There is little doubt that experience in similar situations and a clear vision of the future contribute to the subliminal decision on one course of action versus another, but I doubt the details of the working of the mind will ever become well-enough understood to allow a simple procedure for it to be written. We may see some artificial intelligence systems (expert systems) developed that can do a reasonably good job on some classes of problems. I believe one factor that helps managers who make intuitive decisions is that they become committed to the success of their decision, something a piece of paper or computer can never do. A book by Miller provides a good review and summary of the field as it currently is understood (34). An American and a Japanese author have teamed up to produce a book that suggests that the ideal solution is to combine the best features of the rational and intuitive approaches (35).

References

1. Jeffrey W. Marr, "Letting the Customer Be the Judge of Quality," *Quality Progress* 19(10):46–49 (October 1986).

2. Howard Schuman and Stanley Presser, *Questions and Answers in Attitude Surveys: Experiments on Question Form,*

Wording, and Context (Orlando, FL: Academic Press, 1981), pp. 1–5.

3. *Webster's New Collegiate Dictionary* (Springfield, MA: G & C Merriam, 1981).

4. Genichi Taguchi, *Introduction to Quality Engineering: Designing Quality Products and Processes* (White Plains, NY: Quality Resources, 1986).

5. George E. P. Box and Norman R. Draper, *Evolutionary Operation: A Statistical Method for Process Improvement* (New York: John Wiley, 1969).

6. George E. P. Box and Soren Bisgaard, "The Scientific Context of Quality Improvement," *Quality Progress* 20(6):54–61 (June 1987).

7. W. A. Shewhart, *Economic Control of Quality of Manufactured Product* (New York: Van Nostrand, 1931), pp. 37–54.

8. Irving W. Burr, *Statistical Quality Control Methods* (New York: Marcel Dekker, 1976).

9. Eugene L. Grant and Richard S. Leavenworth, *Statistical Quality Control*, 5th ed. (New York: McGraw-Hill, 1980).

10. Douglas C. Montgomery, *Introduction to Statistical Quality Control* (New York: John Wiley, 1985), pp. 1–19.

11. David C. Hoaglin, Fredrick Mosteller, and John W. Tukey, eds., *Exploring Data Tables, Trends, and Shapes* (New York: John Wiley, 1985).

12. SAS Institute, *SAS® Introductory Guide for Personal Computers*, Version 6 Edition (Cary, NC: SAS Institute, 1985).

13. Stuart L. Meyer, *Data Analysis for Scientists and Engineers* (New York: John Wiley, 1975), pp. 499–504.

14. Edward R. Tufte, *The Visual Display of Quantitative Information* (Cheshire, CT: Graphics Press, 1983).

15. John M. Chambers, et al., *Graphical Methods for Data Analysis* (Boston: Duxbury Press, 1983).

16. WordPerfect Corporation, *WordPerfect® for IBM® Personal Computers and PC Networks* (Orem, UT: WordPerfect Corporation, 1989).

17. Software Publishing Corporation, *Harvard® Graphics: User's Guide* (Mountain View, CA: Software Publishing Corporation, 1990).

18. Thomas P. Ryan, *Statistical Methods for Quality Improvement* (New York: John Wiley, 1989), p. 274.

19. Kaoru Ishikawa, *Guide to Quality Control*, 2nd ed., rev. (Tokyo: Asian Productivity Organization, 1986).

20. Banner Blue, *OrgPlus™ Advanced: User's Guide* (Fremont, CA: Banner Blue, 1988).

21. John E. Ullmann, Donald A. Christman, and Bert Holtje, eds., *Handbook of Engineering Management* (New York: John Wiley, 1986).

22. WST Corporation, *OPEN PLAN® User Guide* (Houston: WST Corporation, 1989).

23. Shigeru Mizuno, ed., *Management for Quality Improvement: The Seven New QC Tools* (Cambridge, MA: Productivity Press, 1988).

24. John R. Hauser and Don Clausing, "The House of Quality," *Harvard Business Review* 66(3):63–73 (May–June 1988).

25. Lawrence P. Sullivan, "Policy Management through Quality Function Deployment," *Quality Progress* 21(6):18–20 (June 1988).

26. Ronald M. Fortuna, "Beyond Quality: Taking SPC Upstream," *Quality Progress* 21(6):23–28 (June 1988).

27. Charles H. Clark, *Brainstorming: The Dynamic New Way to Create Successful Ideas* (Garden City, NY: Doubleday, 1958).

28. Alvin Zander, *Making Groups Effective* (San Francisco: Jossey-Bass, 1983).

29. Andre L. Delbecq, Andrew H. Van de Ven, and David H. Gustafson, *Group Techniques for Program Planning: A Guide to Nominal Group and Delphi Processes* (Glenview, IL: Scott, Foresman, 1975).

30. Gabriele Lusser Rico, *Writing the Natural Way: Using Right-Brain Techniques to Release Your Expressive Powers* (Los Angeles: J. P. Tarcher, 1983).

31. Willis Harman and Howard Rheingold, *Higher Creativity: Liberating the Unconscious for Breakthrough Insights* (Los Angeles: J. P. Tarcher, 1984).

32. Weston H. Agor, "How Top Executives Use Their Intuition to Make Important Decisions," *Business Horizons* 29(1): 49–53 (January–February 1986).

33. Charles H. Kepner and Benjamin B. Tregoe, *The New Rational Manager* (Princeton, NJ: Princeton Research Press, 1981).

34. William C. Miller, *The Creative Edge: Fostering Innovation Where You Work* (Reading, MA: Addison-Wesley, 1987).

35. Gerald Nadler and Shozo Hibino, *Breakthrough Thinking* (Rocklin, CA: Prima Publishing and Communications, 1990).

Chapter 7

Applying the Quality Model

In this chapter, the complete quality model (CQM) presented in Chapter 5 is used to develop useful quality programs for research and development organizations. The six systems that comprise the model (preparation, execution, evaluation, reward, improvement, and correction) are discussed individually. Many of the details discussed in this chapter are based on simple, commonsense management principles, a perspective that sometimes is overlooked in the research and development environment. The model can be used to help define a quality program for anything from a small task, such as presenting a technical paper at a meeting, to a multimillion dollar research and development program. This chapter focuses on the middle ground, the tasks that involve only one or a few people. Activities of this size are the building blocks of larger programs, with the smaller tasks just miniature versions of the same approach.

One of the problems of applying quality principles to research and development activities in the past came from attempting to apply concepts developed and used in the manufacturing world directly to the research and development world. The material in this chapter should prove useful in the research and development environment and should show how to solve quality problems and achieve results.

In developing the components of a quality program, I give one or two examples of how some task might be accomplished. An example points out *a* solution, not *the* solution. Each manufacturing organization has discovered that the correct quality program must be tailored to its organization and environment, and the same need exists in each research and development organization.

The Work to be Done

Because the purpose of this chapter is to show how to put the model to work, the first task is to describe the work to be done. The shaded part of the CQM in Fig. 7.1 serves as a guide. At the start of any activity, you need to define what you are trying to accomplish (the output of the execution system), for whom you are working (the receivers), what resources are required (the input to the preparation system), and what processes or methods are involved in the execution system. Although I will go through the steps of developing a quality program linearly, in an actual application the process usually turns out to be highly iterative. The first work to be done is part of the preparation system. After an initial pass at defining the outputs, receivers, resources, and methods, the remaining systems in the CQM are discussed. In practice, as the other systems are considered, you probably will want to go back and forth and modify sections as new ideas arise. This approach really should not come as much of a surprise to research and development professionals because it is a common method of attack in technical programs.

Outputs. The development of any program should begin with the focus on identification of the outputs: the deliverables, the products, or the results of the task. The main product should be identified first. If there is a goal statement for the project, that should help identify the main product. For research tasks, typical outputs might be: "A correlation of Variable A with Variable

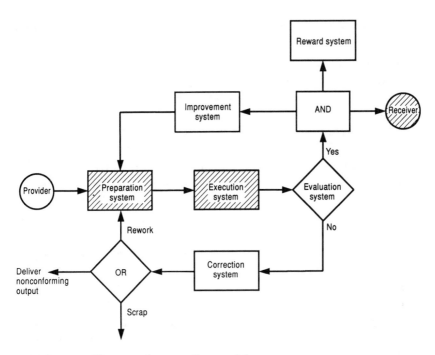

FIGURE 7.1. The complete quality model.

B"; "The rate constant for reaction of Reagent C with Reagent D"; "The infrared spectrum of Compound E"; or, "An analysis of early pottery from Site F."

The primary outputs from research activities should be science, that is, new information or knowledge. Development projects should deliver technology. Examples of the outputs of development tasks are: "A ceramic that will withstand Compound G at temperatures of greater than $H°$ Kelvin"; "A compound that will remain liquid at $-J°$ Fahrenheit"; "An electrical circuit that will have an impedance of K ohms at L gigahertz"; or, "A software program that will sort M records in less than N milliseconds."

Receivers. The next logical step in developing a quality program is to determine who are the receivers of these outputs. The model for people presented in Chapter 5 is helpful in defining all the possibilities. The main output typically will go from a researcher to a developer and from the developer to a designer. Occasionally, the output will go directly to an operations unit. The technical information also should go to the appropriate technical community, proprietary and national security issues permitting. People engaged in experimental work these days must be particularly aware who receives the wastes created by their work. If the work involves materials covered by such acts of legislation as the Clean Water Act, the Resource Conservation and Recovery Act, or the Toxic Substances Control Act, special care must be taken to handle and dispose of these materials properly and also to maintain certain work-related documents and provide copies to the regulatory agencies.

Finally, one receiver common to every task, and to me the most important one, is the person doing the work. One of the most significant aspects of technical work is the personal satisfaction derived by the worker. This fact should be realized at the beginning of the project and should be a factor in the accomplishment of the work. There is nothing wrong with expecting to be satisfied by your work and asking, What's in it for me?

Inputs. The next area to consider in the development of a program is that of the inputs required. All six categories described in Chapter 5 (people, things, time, money, information, and energy) should be considered. The most important inputs are the people required to do the work. These people should include both the immediate staff and the personnel in support organizations. The list of people should include those involved in generating all the outputs, not just the main one.

Next in importance is the category of things required. These things usually include the facilities and equipment, materials and supplies, and any support equipment, such as computers. The third category is information. Virtually all technical activities build on prior work, and the information that has been created already is vital to the success of later work.

For most projects the categories of time, energy, and money are of secondary importance. Budgets and schedules, of course, are necessary, but normally do not drive the science or technology. Energy considerations are usually of minor concern, although their importance is increasing.

Processes. The final aspect of the program definition is to identify and describe the way in which the work will be done. This part is often the most difficult because of the need to identify the processes used to transform the inputs to outputs. The three categories discussed above (outputs, receivers, and inputs) represent things and, in most cases, are reasonably tangible entities. To use a slightly different analogy from that in Chapter 5, the inputs and outputs can be considered as defining the initial and final states of a system (see Fig. 7.2). The process itself then resembles a thermodynamic process since it is the means by which the inputs are transformed into the outputs.

The objective in defining a process is to identify the key steps required to accomplish the transformation. The most useful tools for developing descriptions of processes are the flowchart and its cousin, the work-breakdown structure. These

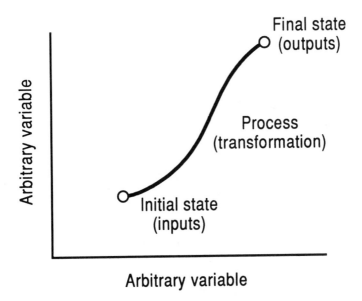

FIGURE 7.2. An analogy between a thermodynamic process and the execution process.

tools require the rigorous examination of the sequence of steps involved in accomplishing the mission. In the next section, some additional material is given to help understand the details of describing the processes.

An expanded perspective on systems. In addition to the main inputs, processes, and outputs (there may be more than one of each), there also may be others that need to be considered. Figure 7.3 illustrates the multiple elements that may be present in the various systems of the CQM. Using this expanded version of the model, the most common administrative outputs from any technical program are the documentation that describes the primary output, such other programmatic documentation as progress reports, results of safety and housekeeping programs, outcomes from financial and personnel actions, and deliverables from facility and equipment actions. Waste products may or may not be an issue, depending on the nature of the

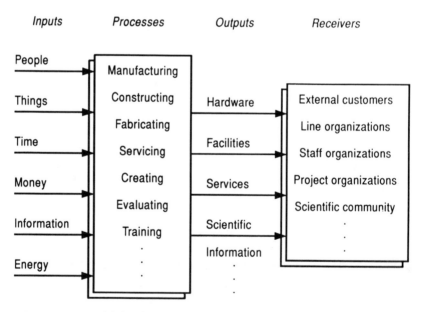

FIGURE 7.3. Multiple elements of the various systems of the complete quality model.

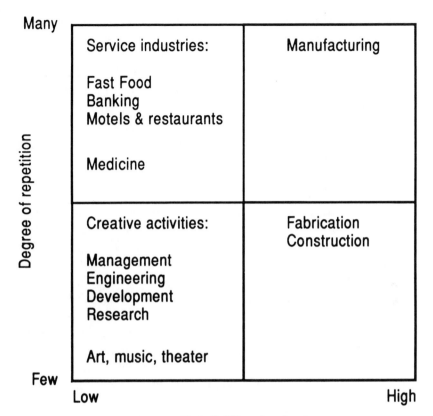

FIGURE 7.4. Repetition–tangibility diagram for industries.

program. If they are, it behooves the technical person to become informed of any pertinent laws or organizational rules so that the wastes can be handled properly.

Action plans, experimental plans, and procedures. Processes can be divided into two classes, steady-state and transient. Steady-state processes typically are found in mature, repetitive operations, the kinds of situations in most manufacturing and service activities. These are the parts of the industrial world depicted in the upper quadrants of Fig. 7.4. For these conditions, the processes involved are described most easily in terms of standard practice procedures or standard operating procedures. Every output should be identical to every other output, and the processes used to produce the outputs should not vary. Although there are aspects of research and development activities that require standardized procedures, the main activity is not amenable to detailed standard procedures. One could argue that the scientific method is the standard procedure for doing all research. While this is true in general, using such a generic concept as the scientific method is not much help because the details of what is done in research and development activities vary from project to project.

The nature of research and development work is intrinsically transient in nature. Research and development activities usually have discrete beginnings and ends. Even programs that continue for long periods can be subdivided (and usually should be subdivided) into segments with well-defined starts and completions. One of the side benefits of using the CQM is the necessity to divide the work into manageable packets. This subdivision is useful to the technical staff as well to the managers of the work. For one thing, it eliminates the feeling of drifting that often occurs in research and development programs with only vague, long-term objectives. A set of intermediate objectives provides some landmarks to use on the journey.

In contrast to steady-state activities, transient activities are described most easily in terms of plans, such as experimental plans, project plans, or action plans, rather than standardized procedures. Attempting to describe projects with standardized procedures instead of action plans is an example of using the wrong tool to handle a problem. A neophyte might make some erroneous simplifying assumptions so that it appeared a solution was found when, in reality, the wrong problem was solved.

Personal and organizational charters. When all the information above concerning inputs, outputs, receivers, and processes has been assembled, you are ready to prepare charters for the people involved in the work and the organizations to which they belong. A suggested general format is given in Fig. 7.5. There is nothing sacred about this format; if your company has its own,

---

POSITION CHARTER

Position: Date:

Incumbent:

The purpose of this position is to provide *(goods and services - OUTPUT)*:

To *(Customers)*:

For *(Budget)*:

By *(Schedule - Milestone Dates)*:

Utilizing *(Resources - INPUT)*:
    Personnel

    Facilities

    Equipment

    Materials and supplies

    Information

Subject to the following considerations:
    Safety

    Quality

Standards used for evaluation:

FIGURE 7.5. General format of a charter.

then that is obviously the one to use. Once this information is assembled, it can be used as the basis for the performance review of individuals in most organizations because it describes what the individual is expected to do, for whom, how, and with what resources.

Concerning the organization, an organizational charter

provides a basis for developing budget requests and setting schedules. In addition, the information can be used to prepare mission statements for a task, project, or program.

The documents described above are called by a variety of names, and each company has its own preference as to format and content. The key point from a quality standpoint is that, before it is possible to define a quality program, it is crucial for the individuals to understand what their part is in the program, what the program is about, and what is the function of their organization. The best way to understand these issues is to commit them to writing.

We have defined what we as individuals and the organizations to which we belong are trying to accomplish and what the products of our tasks are. This information is the basis of simple, commonsense management practice, nothing more. In the next step, we begin to apply the quality perspective to the effort.

Evaluation: The Key to Quality

What transforms otherwise normal management activities into a quality-oriented program is the recognition that everything we do is judged by many people, according to many criteria. If we want to succeed, we need to understand how these evaluations are done and then take deliberate steps to manage the evaluations and not have them manage us by some vague undefined process. We adopt this perspective almost intuitively in such activities as athletics and parlor games in which the rules are known, they are usually simple and straightforward, and the process of evaluation is understood to the point of being trivial. The concept of evaluation is almost as straightforward in most manufacturing, construction, and fabrication environments. The standards are defined by plans and specifications, the testing methods are spelled out clearly, and the pass/fail criteria are known.

This approach to evaluation, with well-defined criteria and evaluation methods, is not as common in most commercial areas outside of manufacturing, especially research and development. As a result, when beginning a quality program in a research or development organization, there are two primary tasks to accomplish in connection with the evaluation system: identifying the standards for the outputs, and determining methods of evaluating the outputs against these standards.

Identifying standards. If asked to come up with the standards for winning a game of Monopoly, you would get a Monopoly set and read the rule book. If asked the same question for a college basketball game, a call to the appropriate National Collegiate Athletic Association office would produce a set of rules. Manufacturers of threaded fasteners could find the requirements for their products in the standards of the American Society of Mechanical Engineers and the Society of Automotive Engineers. While no analogous National Society of Researchers and Developers exists to promulgate standards for research and development output, there are sources for this kind of information. Some of the best sources are in the requirements for publication for professional journals and in texts on writing technical reports (1–3). These sources are useful on two important levels: they define both the form and the substance of the information. One standard for any technical activity is that the results be fit for their intended use. This criterion has been used as a definition of quality. I suggest this usage is incorrect; fitness for intended use is a standard for an output, not a definition of the field itself. Fitness is a key requirement and one that too often is not met.

In basic research, the fundamental standards for the knowledge produced are essentially that the information be original, new, or innovative, that it be well described and documented, that the experimental results be reproducible, that the information be consistent with related information or with any differences clearly explained, and that the information be fit for its intended use. These should be considered as general guidelines only and each activity, each worker, and each organization will need to interpret them for the individual situation.

Applied research should consider these basic criteria along

with whatever specific requirements are added for the information sought. By identifying these criteria, research workers in industrial settings can work wonders in avoiding the trap of over-researching a problem and earning the deserved reputation of living in an ivory tower. If the research organization and the organization requesting the work can arrive at a common set of criteria, both will be happier. By understanding each others' needs and constraints, the work often can be optimized to the benefit of both organizations.

When an organization starts to consider the application of quality principles in technical areas and begins to develop a set of standards for research and development, several of the quality tools described in Chapter 6 can be of assistance. The tools for generating ideas obviously are helpful; brainstorming, the nominal group technique, the Delphi method, and analogs are some that I have used effectively.

Once the idea of defining standards for research and development has been tried out and accepted, the approach usually is found to be relatively simple and can be applied easily to other aspects of an organization. Consider the following examples. We have examined the functions of secretaries and broken down their work into such activities as typing reports, answering phones, and relaying messages. The standards for typing reports are found in secretarial handbooks, style guides, and manuals produced by many companies. The phone company has guidelines and teaches courses on competence and etiquette for answering phones. Standards for relaying messages to staff members were negotiated between the secretaries and the staff. Not only did this help in arriving at a set of mutually agreed-on standards, it also helped each group achieve a broader understanding of the others' needs and constraints.

When the concept of evaluation is applied to managers' functions, they can be broken down into activities like conducting meetings and reviewing and approving documents. The literature contains numerous books and papers on the subject of conducting meetings, and the standards are clear and simple. (One wonders why we still have so much trouble doing it!) The guidelines for reviewing and approving documents should be negotiated between the manager and those for whom he or she is providing the service. Simply discussing what is a reasonable turnaround time and what information should supplement that contained on various forms can streamline an operation and simplify everyone's job.

The identification of criteria also should be done for all the other outputs of the activity. The evaluation process begins with three fundamental steps: deciding on exactly what is to be evaluated, determining what characteristics are significant for the entity to be evaluated, and deciding what values the various characteristics should have. When most people use the terms "requirements," "criteria," or "standards" in the context of the evaluation process, they usually are referring to the combination of characteristic and value; the assumption is that the entity of interest already has been identified. For instance, the standard for a yardstick (entity) is that its length (characteristic) be one yard (value). For many tangible items, deciding on the evaluation criteria is a straightforward process. If you were manufacturing bolts, you obviously would want to evaluate the bolts. Some of the characteristics of interest are the diameter of the bolt and the number of threads per inch. If you were producing 1/4″–20 bolts you would want the diameter to be 0.250 inches (with some appropriate tolerance) and the number of threads to be 20 (again with some appropriate tolerance). The factory in which the bolts were made presumably would have the tools, people, and methods to make the necessary measurements and determine which bolts conformed to the standards and which did not.

Including physical measurements of such characteristics as mass, length, or time, there are basically only five kinds of measurement scales that are needed for any evaluation. These may be called the binary, counting, continuous, rating, and ranking scales. The binary scale is used for evaluations that involve answering such questions as: Does a characteristic exist or not? It is used for situations in which yes/no or on/off answers are needed. The counting scale is used when the numbers of characteristics are of interest; typical uses are to answer questions like: How many beans are in the jar? How many reports were produced last quarter? How many times was this paper cited in the literature? The continuous scale is the one most people think of when dealing with the kind of evaluations called inspections. It is the one applied to most measurements of physical entities and already has been described above. These three scales (binary, counting, and continuous) provide objective information and, in many applications, can be used with completely automatic measuring equipment.

The other two scales, rating and ranking, give subjective information, and must involve humans in their application. Rating scales deal with situations in which you are interested in getting information from such requests as: On a scale of 1 to 5, how would you rate this research project? The usefulness of the rating scales can be improved if they are calibrated. The next paragraph gives an example of this type of calibration. Ranking scales are used when comparisons are needed and handle such situations such as: Compare these three reports and rank them in terms of their readability.

To give some idea of how these various scales can be used in a technical environment, let us consider the evaluation of research reports. Some of the characteristics of interest are the four c's: correctness, completeness, clarity, and conciseness. Correctness should be evaluated on a binary scale: either the information is correct or it is not. No matter how good the rest of the characteristics of the report are, if it fails this test, it is not fit for its intended use. Completeness can be rated from 1 to 5, and it is suggested that anything less than 4 is unacceptable. A 5 would be perfect, 4 could have some sections short or missing or some amount of information deliberately dropped, 3 would indicate significant parts were not present, 2 would imply there were large gaps apparently overlooked in the information, and 1 represents careless, sloppy work. Clarity and conciseness also could be rated from 1 to 5, and again some guidelines (calibration points) for the meaning of the scale values could be given. For this example, professional writers and editors can assist in developing the guidelines. By having this kind of system in place, the authors of technical reports will know ahead of time what is expected of them and can be much more effective in generating documents. Standards for the form of documents are usually straightforward and are defined both by organizations and publishers. With today's electronic methods of document preparation, the dilemma of having inconsistent formats between a company and a journal is much easier to reconcile.

You also should remember to look at the criteria from the receiver's perspective as well as from your own. An operating unit's staff might want just a yes or no answer to a question about some technical issue, while the research staff would prefer to gain an in-depth understanding of the phenomenon to help in future activities. Schedules are often a source of misunderstanding and disagreement between developers and designers. By understanding each other's requirements and constraints at the outset of a project, it should be possible for the development organization to tailor its program to the needs of the design organization. Finally, the requirements for the inputs to the effort need to be identified. If the purpose of the project is to produce silk purses, you need to be sure you are not letting any sow's ears into the system. People in the manufacturing world have learned this lesson just recently and many companies now are working very closely with their suppliers to assure that only materials that conform to standards are introduced into the system.

The discipline that the design profession uses in its requirement for clear and complete design criteria at the beginning of a project is a useful perspective for research and development professionals to adopt. A modern, professional design organization will not begin a design project until it has agreement from the intended receiver of the design on the input criteria and at least some understanding about the nature of the final design.

Evaluating the outputs. The evaluation of the products of knowledge work is more difficult than the evaluation of most other kinds of products because the knowledge-work products are based, at least partially, on subjective criteria in addition to objective requirements. The task of evaluation is complicated further in industrial settings in that there are few, if any, individuals in many companies outside of the research and development organizations who are competent and capable of evaluating the technical aspects of the work.

Nevertheless, at least five individuals or groups will evaluate various aspects of the work, consciously or not, formally or not. One purpose of having a quality program is to identify and formalize these evaluations so their results can be useful to the technical staff. Evaluations are performed by the individual or group that did the work (the doers), the appropriate technical community (the peers), the individual or group that received the information (the receivers), the management of the work (the managers), and groups concerned with the financial, safety, and environmental aspects of the work (the auditors).

Evaluation by the doers. The first level of evaluation can and should be performed by the person or group doing the work. The easiest way to handle this evaluation is to start the preparation of the report by describing the work at the very outset of the project. Committing one's efforts to the written word is the best method I have discovered for testing the correctness and completeness of any piece of work I have ever done. The discipline of writing out the results of a study forces a critical evaluation both of the process by which the results were obtained and of their validity. Anyone who has ever reached the point of preparing a final report of a task and realized there was a major gap in the work quickly learns the value of good planning so that every task is done right the first time.

Peer review. Peer review should begin as early in a project as possible. This type of evaluation can be done by at least three groups: technical peers within the organization, special groups put together just for the purpose of reviewing and evaluating the technical output from an organization (such as advisory boards or review committees), and the technical community. Peer review within an organization can be done formally by having finished reports reviewed before release and informally through the use of small groups of people who are working on the same or related problems. One approach that I have used successfully with technical groups is the technical evaluation and review meeting (TERM) mentioned in Chapter 6. This concept grew out of a desire to have a procedure for improving the method of study as work progressed. For such a procedure to be useful, it had to be simple, not too time consuming (research workers tend to be very selfish about "nonproductive" demands on their time), and it had to be of clear benefit to the program. The meetings were held twice a month and lasted roughly 1 1/2 hours. Initially, the meetings consisted primarily of brief reports by everyone present, followed by one or two longer reports on activities that were at points of completion or that were experiencing difficulties. As more meetings were held, a few dominant themes emerged and the discussions tended to center about those topics. Also, the TERMs often served as the catalyst for additional one-on-one or small-group meetings on important topics; considerable individual and collaborative work was done as a result of these meetings and in preparation for the next TERM.

The particular situation will determine which type of evaluation or which combination of evaluations is most appropriate for any given situation. If you are fortunate enough to be in an organization that is large enough to have a group of peers in-house, then an evaluation by peers is relatively simple, if not completely without apprehension. Universities, major government laboratories, and research and development facilities of companies of Fortune 500 size generally have enough personnel in the major disciplines of interest to the organizations to allow a worker to find a few kindred souls to review his or her work. In fact, in some organizations, this is a regular, normal part of the business. The approach will depend on the nature of the work and the organization. In some cases, the evaluation will come in the form of discussion at a seminar presented by the worker; in others, it can be comments on a report prepared by the worker. If a formal program does not exist and an organization is attempting to institute a comprehensive quality program, one should be started.

If the organization is large enough, it may enjoy the luxury of having an advisory board or review committee to look over its work. When properly utilized, such a group can give useful feedback on the nature and direction of the work underway, provide ideas for new avenues of work, and serve as a sounding board for both technical and administrative issues.

External peer review is the type of evaluation with which most technical people are familiar, and consists basically of submitting a written record of one's work to a journal that has the paper reviewed by several (usually from one to three) technical peers before publication. For the individual in smaller organizations, this type of review and evaluation may be the only kind readily available. Whenever possible, however, this mode of evaluation should be used in conjunction with the in-house evaluation, not instead of it. In some cases, additional review comes when the paper is presented at a technical meeting and the results and conclusions are discussed.

Although external peer review is very important from the perspective of maintaining the overall quality of information in the technical literature, it comes only after the work is completed. For that reason, I strongly recommend a quality program that includes internal peer review so that a task can be kept on track and continuous improvements in methods and results can be achieved.

The evaluations discussed so far have been only of the technical content of the work, the substance. Assuming the document will be used to transmit the information gained from the technical work to the appropriate receivers, the next evaluation of the work should concern the form of the information. This evaluation can be done by a supervisor, secretary, or editor, depending on the nature of the organization involved. The key requirements here are that the spelling, punctuation, and grammar are correct, that the document is in the appropriate format, and that the material is complete and comprehensible.

Numerous good books on technical writing can be of assistance, and software is available that not only will check spelling, but also can check punctuation and grammar and give a readability index. Tools such as these should be used for what they are (helpful tools) and not as absolute criteria for evaluation. Some information never can be presented at a third-grade level, and it is inappropriate to expect a technical person to produce a document that can be understood at that level. For example, this book is intended for an audience that has a college education or the equivalent, and the language is designed for that group.

In this discussion of evaluations, it is assumed that the worker is conscientious and ethical. Errors discovered but not identified, shortcuts deliberately taken, or altered data are fairly easy to hide from outsiders, but not from oneself. Unfortunately, as pressure to publish and competition for funding increases, there are a few unethical people publishing false technical information. The whole issue of evaluating technical information for fraud is just beginning; Refs. 4 and 5 provide more information on this topic.

Receiver review. The next type of evaluation comes in the form of feedback from the receivers of the work. In basic research, the primary receiver is the technical community, and the feedback comes from the external peer review discussed above. The information produced during an applied research investigation usually will go either to a development organization or to a design department; in some industrial settings, the developers and the researchers are the same. Because of this situation, many people think of research and development as one activity, when they should be recognized as two distinct functions with fundamentally different kinds of outputs, receivers, and standards for evaluation. The output from development activities generally is received by a design organization or an operations organization.

The receivers, whoever they may be, will evaluate the work provided to them whether the providers ask them to or not. The benefit of having a proactive quality program is that the provider has a means of determining the receivers' requirements and standards a priori. Thus, the provider can use the requirements to plan his or her program, and obtain useful feedback to help improve the program, and the communication between provider and receiver will be improved. The level of sophistication of the receiver's evaluation depends primarily on the magnitude of the effort involved and the working relation-

ship between receiver and provider. I strongly recommend that
there be some formal evaluation in all cases, regardless of how
well and how long the persons involved have known each other, how well the outputs met everyone's expectations, and how
big the effort was. No activity is so small that its quality may be
neglected. The format for evaluations can range from a simple
questionnaire, to the minutes of an evaluation meeting, all the
way to a formal document summarizing a comprehensive evaluation activity carried out by an independent internal evaluation
group.

*Management evaluation: the individual performance re-
view.* Most companies these days have performance-evaluation
systems of one form or another. Properly done, this kind of
evaluation system can provide additional useful feedback to the
technical worker. These evaluations usually are done by supervisors who may not be skilled in the technical area of the people they are evaluating. The evaluators, however, should be
competent managers and their feedback should be focused on
the nontechnical portion of the work. If the managers are not
competent in the workers' technical fields, the managers
should call upon technical experts within the organization, the
receivers of the technical workers' outputs, and any other
sources available, for assistance in evaluating the technical contributions of the technical workers.

Audits. Workers in large companies and government-
related laboratories often are audited by a variety of internal and
external agencies, especially if their work involves hazardous or
radioactive materials, unusual safety concerns, or large sums of
money. This type of evaluation concentrates on the administrative, rather than the technical, aspects of the program. Unless
these evaluations are handled properly, they can become time
consuming and disruptive. The information gained from the
findings of these evaluations can be useful to technical organizations in determining how to operate their programs so as to be
in compliance with various laws and regulations, thus avoiding
problems with regulatory agencies. If a technical group is to be

audited on the nontechnical aspects of its program, it is generally a good idea to enlist the aid of specialists in the area to be audited, both to assure compliance with the auditors' requirements and to minimize impact on the technical program.

Rewards and Recognition

Although some organizations have had reward and recognition systems that acknowledged outstanding performance, the idea now being promoted in the quality industry of rewarding large numbers of workers is causing discomfort to some traditional managers who believe that people's salaries are all the reward they deserve. In the past, recognition systems have included the Nobel Prize for outstanding performance in a variety of areas, company programs that identify the top fraction of a percent of performers, and university programs that recognize outstanding faculty members. At the other end of the reward scale, it always has been recognized that everybody likes a pat on the back.

For a reward and recognition system to be appropriate and meaningful to a technical organization, it should focus on the contributions of individuals and groups to the quality objectives of the organization. An organization may have other reward programs relating to sales volume, technical achievement, or teaching ability, but the one of interest here should be related only to the quality program. Ideally, all of the reward programs in an organization should be coordinated and may even feed one another, but the quality reward program should stay focused on the quality program.

If an organization is going to ask all of its members to participate in a quality program, the organization needs to be willing and ready to acknowledge everyone's efforts and not just those of an outstanding few. The problem of broad-based recognition is particularly difficult in technical organizations for two reasons. First, because it is a new idea, the introduction of such a program often will be met with the usual skepticism and doubt that is common among technical people. A typical reaction will be to view the program as another trick to get more work out of the staff. The second reason broad-based recognition is difficult is that many technical people tend to be on the shy side and shun being singled out. In my experience, I have observed technical people to decline recognition, saying they were reluctant to appear overly ambitious or to claim more recognition than their co-workers.

One approach to a reward system that is appropriate for technical organizations is to use it as a means to celebrate accomplishments. Everybody loves a party and any excuse for having one will do. Quality recognitions can be like birthday parties. All the members of the organization gather together to celebrate someone's accomplishments. Everyone participates and a few people are the honorees.

Continuous Improvement in a System with Only One Output

The concept of continuous improvement originated in mass-production environments, and attempts now are being made to apply it to many other areas. In a mass-production environment, the concept implies that each item produced will be better than the last in terms of quality, cost, or reduced waste products. Because research and development are improvement activities the basic objective of which is to effect continuous advances in science and technology, and because research and development projects usually have only one output, the traditional concept of continuous improvement must be modified. The best approach to continuous improvement in research and development activities is to look for ways to monitor the progress of the work constantly so that refinements can be made along the way. Continuous improvement in research and development is a matter of ongoing course correction the first time a path is taken, rather than optimizing a route that already has been established.

Improvements can be of two types: improvements in the knowledge, or improvements in the process used to obtain the knowledge. The first case involves looking at continuous review of the progress of the study and regular evaluation of the state of knowledge acquired. Rather than plan an experimental program, blindly go through all the steps, and finally review all the information to see what was found, a quality-oriented program will review the data and the interpretation of the data regularly to be sure the desired goals are being approached and that an expanded and improved understanding can be obtained. In some cases, a few extra data points taken at the appropriate point in a program will improve the accuracy or range of validity of the results with virtually no additional cost.

The second type of improvement involves continuously reviewing the means by which the work is being conducted. It may be possible to streamline some part of the data-acquisition technique or to use a better algorithm for the reduction of the data. The benefit from an improvement system comes from the regular, deliberate, conscious review of activities being performed to find ways of making small, steady improvements in work methods. Research and development activities are similar to other activities in presenting opportunities for improvement.

As with any constant improvement program, the best people to be involved are the ones actually doing the work. When the project is large enough, the team working on it can meet regularly to review both aspects of the program. The nature of technical work seems to be such that gatherings of 1½ to 2 hours every 2 or 3 weeks seem to be more productive than weekly meetings of an hour or so. However, when work is at the point at which large amounts of data are being acquired, it may be beneficial to meet more frequently to review progress, evaluate results, and plan the next series of experiments.

For research or development activities involving only one person or perhaps a small number of people, colleagues with similar backgrounds and interests within the organization can join together to review each other's work. For this type of review to be useful, a group of between 6 and 20 people is required. Groups smaller than 6 generally do not generate enough diverse views to be creative, and groups larger than 20 are too cumbersome to be productive. For those situations in which a small company has only a modest-size technical staff, a local technical society can provide at least a monthly forum for common interests to be discussed. Even with the restrictions placed by competitive concerns, many of the issues facing technical people can be discussed without compromising a company's industrial secrets.

Correction System

The need to address and correct sporadic problems has been recognized in the quality field for many years. The original concept again dealt with the manufacturing world, in which, for whatever reason, some parameter would start to deviate from its required value. The problem then became to decide whether to rework the out-of-tolerance item, scrap it, or have the customer accept it (probably at a reduced price, but not as a complete loss to the company). In technical work, the problem, again, is being faced by a system with only one main output.

There are three main categories of sporadic problems encountered in technical work: those relating to the work itself, those relating to the technical infrastructure involved, and those relating to the associated administrative systems. The first group includes situations in which the results simply are not what was expected. This may result from inaccuracies in theoretical predictions or from the sometime perverseness of nature. In basic research, this situation often can lead to new insights and new avenues of exploration. The greatest damage is often to the researcher's pride for not having better foreseen the results. If ever there was a classic example of the Chinese philosophy behind the yin-yang symbol, which represents both adversity and opportunity, it is when a researcher finds an anomaly and opens the door to a new way of understanding. The researcher must be able to recognize the opportunity and take advantage of it. However, when similar difficulties are encountered in applied research and development activities, there can be a significant impact on the ensuing stages of product or process development. When this occurs, the technical staff must communicate their findings to everyone else involved in the program so that appropriate adjustments can be made.

The problems related to the technical infrastructure include equipment breaking down, bugs in software, and reagents that do not meet specifications. The types of situations involving administrative problems frequently involve interactions with such support organizations as the maintenance, purchasing, personnel, and finance departments. Typical problems might be the inability of a maintenance organization to repair a piece of experimental equipment because of a sudden, unexpected increase in higher priority work in other parts of the organization, unexpected increases in overhead caused by the need for facility modifications to bring the operation into compliance with new environmental regulations, or the introduction of a new performance-appraisal system that will require additional training and paperwork on the part of the technical staff and their managers. The problems described above, either singly or in combination, often lead to situations in which time or money runs out and the results either are incomplete or not what was expected.

Although most sporadic problems are unique, a few general principles can be useful in establishing a methodology for resolving any problems that do occur. The issues mentioned above are similar to those found in other industrial settings. Some organizations will have formal procedures for handling such problems. In those situations in which procedures already exist, they probably can be used with little or no modification. For organizations that do not have a correction system already in place, the technical organization should establish one. A few simple guidelines for such a system are given below.

The basic components of a correction system are shown in Fig. 7.6. The components include systems for determining the nature and severity of the problems and assigning responsibility for correcting them; for preparing plans to correct the problems and for reviewing the plans and approving their execution; for performing the actual corrections and verifying that they have been performed and performed correctly; and, last but not least, in all but the smallest organizations, a formal system to track the progress on resolution of the problems. A tracking system such as this works best when it is a normal part of the organization's management system. The complexity and degree

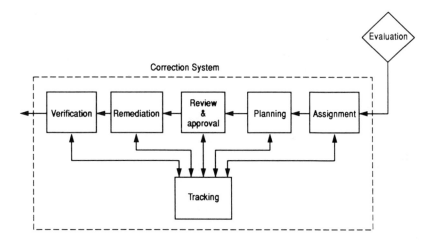

FIGURE 7.6. Components of a correction system.

of formality of these systems will depend on the size of the organization and the nature of the work being done. Each organization will need to tailor its correction system to its particular needs.

Be Prepared

The main aspects of the model are discussed above. Let us now review project preparation and its connection with a parallel quality program. We should understand all of the parts of a quality program and how they fit together before proceeding with any project. To paraphrase an old slogan, If you don't know where you're going, you can't tell how to start getting there.

Good preparation is synonymous with good planning. At the beginning of any task, the first step should be the preparation of a plan for accomplishing the goals of the task. We do this intuitively and informally in any case. Yet, what often distinguishes excellent work from mediocre work is the existence and use of good plans.

First, be sure you understand what you are trying to accomplish, who the receivers are, what resources are needed, and what processes will be used. Figure 7.1 shows the part of the CQM that describes these components and forms the heart of a management model. Simply stating this information on paper in the form of a position charter or mission statement will provide a solid basis for the related program. The document should be reviewed by all the affected parties, such as project personnel, managers, receivers, providers of services and materials, regulators, and members of staff organizations, to be sure that everyone understands and agrees with the main aspects of the charter.

Assuming everyone is in agreement, the next step is to refine the description of the input requirements. Staff members may need to be recruited and trained, materials and equipment may need to be acquired, and facilities may need construction or modification. For each of these and any other significant inputs, plans will need to be developed. When significant actions are involved, a second level, and perhaps even more levels, of details should be generated. For instance, if staff members with special training or skills are required, the application of the model will help prepare the position description that the personnel organization can use in its recruiting efforts. If the project requires an individual with a background in optics, a simple description of the staffing system might state: The purpose of this system is to hire an individual with a Ph.D. degree in physics or a related field with a specialty in optics (the output of the staffing system is the new staff member) who will report to the project manager (the receiver). Only candidates from a selected list of schools with specific grade-point averages will be considered (the inputs). After an initial screening of potential candidates by the project manager and the chief scientist, the top three will be invited for an interview and to give a seminar. The three will be ranked by consensus of the entire staff, and the employment department will make an offer to the top choice (the process used to achieve the objective).

As you can see, the model, so far, is applicable in virtually all situations with only slight variations. The other features of the model also should be applied, especially the evaluation system. In the example described above, the beginnings of the evaluation system are the standards for grade-point average and the process by which the selection was to be made. The standards for the candidates and the process by which they will be evaluated should be thought out and documented in more detail before the actual recruitment is started. It is much easier to ask candidates to come prepared for specific activities or to have them bring certain kinds of documents than to have them handle such requests after a visit, especially if you are looking for individuals with scarce talents.

The same approach should be used to determine the requirements for equipment, facilities, and other major components of a program. Other major considerations in many programs are training requirements and preparation of special procedures when new techniques or pieces of equipment are involved. The degree of formalization will depend on the complexity of the situation and the potential for harm to the workers, the equipment, and the environment.

The preparation phase is the time to ensure that all the requirements of all receivers are understood and agreed upon by the participants. If conflicting requirements exist among different receivers, this is the time to resolve differences. This is also the time to establish how the work is to be evaluated and by whom. If an advisory committee is to be established, now is the time to do it. An advisory committee often can be of particular use in getting a project started on the right track, rather than coming in later and attempting to make a major change in direction.

Basic Research, Applied Research, Development

In this section, the application of the model to basic research, applied research, and development programs is illustrated. Although the details, for the most part, are hypothetical, the examples are based on actual programs.

Basic research. The output of a research project, whether it is basic or applied, is scientific information. The information may be in the form of theories, formulas, correlations, or evaluations of information. Recall that in basic research there are usually no specific receivers outside of the person or group doing the work and the cognizant scientific community.

The place to start the application of the CQM is in the preparation system with the creation of a document that describes the work to be done. Several years ago I was interested in ways of increasing the amount of heat that could be removed from a surface while still limiting the temperature of the surface. Although the idea of the need for the work came from the world of practical applications, there was no specific application in mind at the time and, consequently, there would be no specific requirements for the outcome. Thus, the only standards for a basic research project in this area would be that the work represent good research. A relatively brief mission statement could be used to describe the work, such as that in Fig. 7.7. In this case, the emphasis is on describing the nature of the work to be accomplished and any constraints put on the scope of the work. In any project, even one involving basic research, rather than have a vague statement that covers everything under the sun, I prefer to define the scope of the work rather explicitly. In this example, the scope is limited to the study of heat transfer from round rods to axially flowing fluid and to the influence of wires wrapped spirally around the rods.

A well-structured evaluation system can be of benefit to technical organizations in several ways. An evaluation program should look at both the form and the substance of the work being performed. Evaluations should be made of the science and technology per se, as well as the form in which they are presented. One benefit of having an evaluation system is that it can provide a mechanism for continuous feedback on the quality of the work performance and on the results being obtained. In an organization ranging in size from 10 to 50 members, the feedback could come from the review of regular progress reports by a group of co-workers and from quarterly program reviews by the managers and receivers involved. Another major benefit is the identification of areas for further study and of methods to improve the processes being used to conduct the work. Regular quality-oriented meetings of the technical staff

The purpose of this project is to determine the heat transfer characteristics of six round rods with spirally wrapped wires with air flowing axially inside a cylindrical tube. The primary recipients of the results will be the conceptual reactor design group at the laboratory and the general heat transfer research community. The results will be documented in a detailed internal technical report and in a summary technical paper to be submitted for presentation at the heat transfer conference.

The work will be performed in the gas flow heat transfer system. Six fully instrumented test sections will be needed along with a data acquisition and reduction system. The principal investigator and one technician will be required to perform the construction and experimental phases of the work over a period of one year. An editor and word processor will be needed part time for two months to prepare the documentation.

It is expected that three months will be required to modify the system and have the six test sections fabricated. Acquisition of the experimental data should require six months, and an additional three months will be needed to analyze the data and prepare the documentation.

FIGURE 7.7. Sample mission statement.

should have agenda items to explore areas needing further study consciously and deliberately to improve the understanding of the phenomenon under investigation. Regular reviews also should be conducted of experimental techniques, computing algorithms, and document preparation systems to seek areas that can benefit from improvement.

In addition to the various internal evaluations of the outputs of a research organization, the members of the organization also should utilize the traditional mechanism of submission of articles for peer review and publication in professional journals whenever and wherever possible.

Applied research. A study of the reaction of aluminum with uranium hexafluoride is used to illustrate the difference between a basic and an applied research project. In U.S. gaseous diffusion plants, uranium hexafluoride is used as the process gas, and many of the plant components are made of aluminum. While aluminum is essentially inert with respect to UF_6, under some extreme temperature conditions that might occur during a major accident it is possible for an accelerated reaction to occur between the two materials. In order to perform a comprehensive safety analysis of the process, it was necessary to understand the situation that might occur if the extreme temperature conditions happened. In this instance, in addition to the generic requirements for scientific information, specific limits were imposed on the temperatures and pressures to be studied. In a basic research project, there would be no such limits, and the researcher would be free to investigate whatever parameters were of interest. While the problem definition is usually more specific in applied research, if something unusual showed up in the course of the study, the researcher could recommend that additional studies should be made at a later time, assuming that time and money were available.

One of the important constraints on applied research is the limitation of the work to the immediate problem. Applied research projects commonly have a specific receiver with a specific need. That receiver probably will be interested in the results of the applied research because of either a current problem or an opportunity to explore a new area. The funding for the work may be limited and the time in which the information is needed may be short. Failure to adhere to the restrictions imposed by the receiver can lead to misunderstandings and disputes between the research organizations and the receivers of their outputs.

For this reason, a detailed project charter is more appropriate for the applied research project than a general mission statement. In the project charter, the internal receivers should be identified specifically and the detailed requirements for the output should be identified clearly. In situations in which the receivers are not sure what the requirements should be, the researcher has the obligation to help them define the requirements as concretely as possible. As mentioned above, lack of agreement on specific requirements is a major source of miscommunication.

In addition to the technical requirements, it is also important to understand the schedule and budget constraints that must be accommodated. Careful planning during the preparation phase and incorporation of reasonable cost and schedule contingencies often can avoid the creation of situations in which the required information takes longer to obtain or costs more than the receiver expected.

The applied researcher has a more difficult problem in obtaining good evaluations of his or her work than a person engaged in basic research. Because of some of the limits imposed on the scope of the work, some projects will not be broad enough to warrant publication in a professional journal. In other cases, it may be necessary to protect the information as business sensitive. When outside evaluations are not practical, the various inside evaluations must be utilized as much as possible. Internal seminars, program reviews, progress reports, and topical or final reports are all candidates for use in an evaluation program. The managers and internal receivers, along with co-workers, are the best source of evaluators for applied research projects.

Development. Development projects generate technology as their outputs. Technology can be in the form of a material, a piece of hardware, or the procedure by which to create some entity. Development programs usually have the most definite requirements of the three kinds of activities considered here. In development work, there is usually a specific application in mind and criteria are well defined. By this time in a product's life cycle, the basic science has been defined and the development program now must provide whatever technology is not yet available in the marketplace.

The output of the development phase of a product's life cycle often is crucial to the ultimate success of the program. Up to this point, a new product was characterized mainly by clever ideas and scientific information. It is in the development phase that these good ideas must be translated into tangible products. Very often, the development organization is asked (expected) to make major leaps in progress.

Setting up a useful system for evaluating the output of a development program can be the most difficult of the three types of activities examined here. Often, a major constraint on development work done in a commercial environment is that it must be kept confidential. If the work is successful, the company probably will want to use it to commercial advantage. If it is not successful, there is probably no general interest in the results.

The most important aspect of the evaluation program is the identification of appropriate standards for the development work. The basic standards for good technical work still hold. Unfortunately for the development organization, there are usually only two possible overall evaluations: outstanding, if the technology solved the problem, and unsatisfactory, if it did not. If an answer was found, the receiver probably does not care how well the development work was done, at least at first. If a satisfactory answer was not found, it does not matter how well the work was done because the project probably will be terminated. No one may recognize that the development organization saved the company considerable expense by identifying the flaws in the idea before more funds were committed.

In either case, this emphasizes a fundamental requirement for all development work: the work must be documented carefully and all attempts that failed should be as well documented as those that succeeded. If the work is successful, the project probably will continue. In this case, it is vital that the engineering designers and production people who will have to use the technology have a complete understanding of all the details. It can be very disconcerting (and expensive) to get to the pilot plant stage of a project only to have serious questions about the results of the development work. This is not to say that all scale-up problems can be avoided if only the developers do a better job. There always will be new factors to take into account as the equipment size changes, speeds change, worker skill levels vary, and raw materials are acquired in production quantities rather than laboratory quantities. Nevertheless, the more comprehensive the job done during the development phase, the fewer the problems that are likely to appear in subsequent stages.

If a suitable answer is not found, the need for complete documentation is even greater. If enough interest exists in the idea, work may be resumed at a later date. Complete documentation can help avoid going down the same path again, and also may help new people see where the stumbling blocks were in the original investigation.

Other tasks. In addition to the types of activities described above, research and development people in most organizations often are called upon to perform a wide variety of peripheral tasks. While these activities are valid and necessary to most companies, they are not research or development and therefore should not be handled the same way necessarily. For instance, it is not uncommon for a research chemistry department to be asked to perform chemical analysis for other parts of the organization. These tasks may take more time in a research lab than they would in a standard analytical lab because the research lab probably is not set up to handle this type of work. The internal customers become dissatisfied with both the time required and the cost. When this type of case arises, it is important for both the researcher and the intended receiver to be sure they understand what is involved. In small organizations in which a technical group may be chartered to perform research, development, and service, all the participants should understand the situation.

In another example, a development organization was asked to develop a special coating for a structural component exposed to very high temperatures. When it came time to perform some pilot plant scale tests, the development organization was called upon to produce sizable quantities of the coating over an extended period of time. The nature of the work and the scale of the activity changed significantly. A shift had to be made from laboratory-scale equipment to small-scale production equipment to produce the material. The perspective of the quality program also had to change from one concerned with the development of a single material to a program more typical of a manufacturing operation. By working closely with the receiver, definite schedules and costs that were appropriate to the nature of the development organization yet still coincided with the needs of the pilot plant's operation were developed.

Summary

Because the purpose of any organization is to create an output, the focus of most quality programs primarily will be on the preparation, execution, and evaluation systems. Improvement, correction, and reward systems (when they exist) usually are managed on a companywide level. If a technical organization is to have a complete quality program, it must become familiar with either the appropriate company systems and adapt them to the technical communities' needs or develop systems of their own. Unless an organization is very rigidly controlled, there is generally a fair amount of latitude in how such programs are applied to an individual organization.

The CQM provides a framework for building the six systems that make up a total quality program. All six systems are valuable to technical organizations when properly designed and utilized. However, it is vital to design the systems to fit the needs of the technical organization rather than try to adapt techniques that have evolved from the manufacturing, construction, or service industries. As is the case in attempting to solve most technical problems, the place to start is with first principles.

References

1. Janet S. Dodd, ed., *The ACS Style Guide: A Manual for Authors and Editors* (Washington, DC: American Chemical Society, 1986), pp. 1–2.

2. Robert A. Day, *How to Write and Publish a Scientific Paper*, 2d ed. (Philadelphia: ISI Press, 1979), pp. 90–93.

3. "Instructions for Contributors," *Risk Analysis: An International Journal*, ed. Curtis Travis (New York: Plenum Press). These instructions are printed on the inside back cover of each issue of the journal.

4. Adil E. Shamoo, ed., *Principles of Research Data Audit* (New York: Gordon and Breach, 1989).

5. Adil E. Shamoo, ed., *Accountability in Research, Policies and Quality Assurance* 1(1) (New York: Gordon and Breach, 1989).

In Conclusion

The quality profession is reaching a level of maturity and sophistication that allows it to address issues concerning a wide
variety of fields and a broad range of complexity. The basis of
the field is changing from a set of disconnected, empirical procedures and techniques to an integrated, cohesive science. In
this book, I have shown how a quality program can be structured around a complete quality model and applied to technical
organizations engaged in research or development. A quality
program built on this model is consistent with all the concepts
of quality used today. Although all the classical and modern
quality tools and concepts apply to research and development,
they cannot be used blindly. We must remind ourselves continuously that we should not be using steamrollers to crack
walnuts. Simply because a tool or technique was found to be
valuable in one context does not mean it will be useful in all
other situations. One of the main lessons the reader should gain
from this book is the concept that any quality program should
be developed from first principles, rather than trying to force an
approach that was developed for some other application to fit
the research and development world. Scientists and engineers
have realized the importance of this methodology in their tech-

143

nical fields. It is equally important in related administrative fields. Many of the failures of quality programs, not only in technical areas but in a variety of other areas, are due to the misapplication of good ideas. By starting with the fundamentals, a better program will be produced, and the program will be more rational and reasonable to research and development professionals.

Obviously, in a field as new as the application of quality methods to research and development, there is a need for more work. In terms of the model developed in this book, the most interesting and potentially productive areas for further work are evaluation, reward, and improvement. Finding ways to evaluate technical work is probably the major area in which additional studies should be conducted. Evaluations should help the company or organization paying for the work, and they also should benefit the technical person or persons involved without being, or even appearing to be, limiting or negative. Quality professionals and managers of scientists and engineers must be careful to separate the administrative aspects of a job from the technical aspects when performing evaluations. The evaluators need to understand the nature of technical work well enough to define requirements in terms that are meaningful and acceptable to the technical community.

The scientific and technical professional organizations need to provide forums for the discussion of the meaning of quality in their fields and start developing the quality equivalents of technical consensus standards for scientific and technical products. In addition, the colleges of engineering and science should collaborate with the management schools and industrial engineering departments to address this same issue. The colleges also can begin to offer courses, or at least seminars, in their professional schools to introduce the concepts of quality as applied to technical efforts before their graduates enter "the real world." It would seem that such topics as "Evaluation of Professional Work Based on Consensus Standards" might be interesting ones for research in a variety of schools and departments, including engineering, physics, sociology, business, and education. The concept of peer review needs to be examined as group dynamics has been. Most professionals who are asked to review a paper for a technical journal or to be a member of a Ph.D. review committee are not trained in the peer review process. We scientists seem to believe peer review happens as if by magic when you get two or three people together to look over somebody else's work. The ideas set forth in Chapter 7 provide a starting point for the development of a rational, structured peer review program. It has taken almost 80 years to develop the art and science of metrology to its present state and we still see new measuring products on the market each month. We are not quite so antiquated as to use the "thickness of a worn shilling" as our standard for technical work, but almost. It will take time to develop a set of gauge blocks for science and engineering and then train everyone how to use them and accept the fact that they are beneficial.

Another source of research relating to the application of quality principles to technical work is in the area of rewarding individuals and groups for their contributions. Managers need to have an assortment of reward and recognition programs at their disposal. In contrast to a sales department, where contributions are easily quantifiable and the impact of the contribution on the success of the business is obvious, the benefit to a company from research or development programs is harder to quantify and of less immediate obviousness. Nevertheless, the impact may be very significant in the future. That being the case, reward and recognition systems should be developed that recognize contributions as much for their immediate scientific and technical merit as for their potential future economic benefit.

Technical people also need to learn to be gracious and grateful recipients. Some of the difficulties with recognition programs in the past have stemmed from false modesty on the part of some technical people, and other problems have been due to petty jealousy on the part of co-workers. As the quality ethic spreads, it is hoped that these problems will diminish and all workers can share in one another's accomplishments and celebrate their achievements together.

The final area needing additional study is in the application of the concept of continuous improvement to processes with only one output, of which research and development are typical examples. Even though there is only one product, there are processes and procedures used in the creation of that product that are repeated, and these should be the subject of some study. The emphasis in activities with singular outputs should be on doing it right the first time. In order to do something right the first time, it is important to have all the processes that are involved in the production of that product under control. In technical work, that requires instruments to be calibrated, references to be verified, and intermediate results to be peer reviewed. No one has devised the perfect calibration system, reference verification technique, or peer review process yet, so there is still room for improvement.

This is an exciting and enjoyable time for the quality profession and for those involved with it. One of the main attractions of science and engineering is the opportunity to be at the leading edge of new discoveries and to be able to apply old ideas to new tasks. As science and technology become more complex, as technical achievements become more costly to achieve, and as the impact of science and technology on our lives becomes more significant, assuring the quality of the results we produce is vital. The economic impact of foreign competition is already significant and will increase as European nations consolidate their forces and as more third-world countries move into the 20th century. The domain of quality must extend to all aspects of our activities if we want to stay at the forefront of innovation and improvement. Research and development, based on already high standards, are the foundation on which our society is built, and the time is ripe to begin the methodical search for ways to find and achieve even more challenging standards.

Index